TOWER AIR FRYER COOKBOOK

365-Day Crispy, Easy and Affordable Recipes for Your Whole Family and Friends with Tips & Tricks to Fry, Grill, and Bake.

Copyright©2023 **Rosie Williams**
All rights reserved. No part of this book may be reproduced or used in any manner without the prior written permission of the copyright owner, except for the use of brief quotations in a book review.
First paperback edition May 2023.
Cover art by Natalie M. Kern
Printed by Amazon in the USA.
Disclaimer : Although the author and publisher have made every effort to ensure that the information in this book was correct at press time, the author and publisher do not assume and hereby disclaim any liability to any party for any loss, damage, or disruption caused by errors or omissions, whether such errors or omissions result from negligence, accident, or any other cause. this book is not intended as a substitute for the medical advice of physicians.

CONTENTS

INTRODUCTION 6

DESSERTS RECIPES 11

Roasted Pears & Shortbread 11
Cranberry Orange Sweet Rolls 11
Air-fryer Chocolate Swirl Meringues 12
Peppermint Cookies 13
Air Fried Marshmallow Peeps 13
Easy Air Fryer Donuts 13
Bratapfe With Vanilla Sauce 14
Air-fryer Peaches 14
Air-fryer Hot-cross-bun Ice-cream Balls ... 14
St Patrick's Day Air Fryer Oven Cupcakes . 15
How To Make Apple Pie Bombs 15
Air Fryer Homemade Cannoli 16
Maple Roasted Acorn Squash 17
Lemon Meringue Cupcakes 17
Air Fryer Oreo 18
Air-fryer Apple Fritters 18
Cinnamon Apple Oatmeal Dog Treats 18
Air Fryer Grilled Cheese 19
Cherry Hand Pies 19
Shrunken Apple Punch 20
Air Fryer Bananas 20
Halloween Cupcakes 21
Vortex Air Fryer French Toast Bake 21
Air Fryer Blueberry Scones 22
Air Fryer Gingersnap Cookies 22

BREAKFAST & BRUNCH RECIPES 23

Air Fryer Breakfast Sandwiches 23
Breakfast Oat Cake 23
Frozen Egg Rolls In The Air Fryer 23
Air Fryer Bacon 24
Air Fryer Hash Brown Egg Bites 24
Air Fried Easy Breakfast Pastries 25
Air Fryer French Toast 25
Easy Air Fryer Pizza Roll Ups 25
Air Fryer Bread 26
Fried Egg In The Air Fryer 26
Air Fryer Cinnamon Roll Bites 26
Air Fryer Pizza Egg Rolls 27
Air Fryer Eggs 27
Air Fryer Pasta Tacos 28
Air Fryer Churros 28
Air Fried Peanut Butter Cups 29
Air Fried Breakfast Muffins 29
Air Fryer Copycat Starbucks Bread 29
Air Fryer French Onion Corn 30
Air Fryer Blueberry Baked Oats 30
Air Fryer Egg Rolls 31
Air Fryer Brisket Tacos 31
Air Fryer Avocado Eggs 31
Air Fryer Zucchini Pizza Bites 32
Air Fryer Mini Egg And Cheese Quiche ... 32

BEEF, PORK & LAMB RECIPES 33

Air Fryer Bacon Wrapped Corn 33
Air Fryer Pork Chops In 9 Minutes 33
Air Fryer Bbq Chops 33
Air Fryer Bacon Wrapped Dates 34
Air Fryer Roast Pork Belly 34
3-ingredient Air Fryer Crescents 35

Air Fryer Taco Casserole 35
Air Fryer Prosciutto Wrapped Asparagus . 35
Air Fryer Bacon Wrapped Sprouts............ 36
Air Fryer Armadillo Eggs 36
Air Fryer Taco Ring 37
Air Fryer Korean-inspired Pork................. 37
Air Fryer Bacon Sprouts 38
Air Fryer Steak Bites.................................. 38
Air Fryer Herb Crusted Roast Beef........... 38
Air Fryer Boneless Pork Chops 39
Air Fryer Ham Steaks................................. 39
Air Fryer Candied Bacon........................... 40
Air Fryer Bacon... 40
Air Fryer Chuck Roast 40
Air Fryer Corn Ribs 41
Ribs.. 41
Air Fryer Steak.. 42
Air Fryer Short Ribs.................................. 42
Air Fryer Ham With Pineapple Glaze....... 43
Air Fryer Brown Sugar Pork Chops 44
Air Fryer Crispy Chilli Beef...................... 44
Air Fryer Beef Empanadas........................ 44
Air Fryer Bacon Wrapped Serranos.......... 45
Air Fryer Grilled Ham And Cheese........... 45

SANDWICHES & BURGERS RECIPES 46
Keto Friendly Game Day Burgers 46
Air Fryer Hamburgers 46
Air Fried Crispy Chicken Sandwiches....... 46
Air Fryer Grilled Cheese Sandwich........... 47
Air Fryer Bacon, Egg................................. 47
Air Fryer Frozen Burger 48
Air Fryer Chicken Burgers 48
Greek Lamb Burgers................................. 48
Air Fryer Biscuit Egg Sandwiches............ 49

FISH & SEAFOOD RECIPES 50
Air Fryer Honey Mustard Salmon 50
Air Fryer Mahi Mahi.................................. 50
Air Fryer Oven Cheesy Potatoes 51
Air Fryer Crispy Fish Fillets...................... 51
Air Fryer Fried Shrimp 52
Frozen Shrimp In The Air Fryer 52
Air Fryer Coconut Shrimp 53
Air Fryer Lobster Tail 53
Cajun Air Fryer Fish 53
Air Fryer Scallops...................................... 54
Fish 'n' Chips... 54
Air-fryer Salmon With Teriyaki Glaze 55
Crisp-skinned Air Fryer Salmon 55
Air Fryer Shrimp 55
Air Fryer Shrimp Skewers 56
Air Fryer Breaded Shrimp 56
Air Fryer Fish Tacos.................................. 57
Air Fryer Tuna Patties 57
Air-fried Beer Battered Fish Tacos 58
Air Fryer Calamari.................................... 58
Air Fryer Salmon And Swiss Chard 59
Air Fryer Bacon Wrapped Shrimp............ 59
Air-fryer Fish Tacos 60
Air Fryer Cod 60
Air Fryer Blackened Mahi Mahi 61
Air Fryer Salmon With Maple Soy Glaze...61

POULTRY RECIPES ... 62

- Chicken Sausage In The Air Fryer 62
- How To Reheat Fried Chicken 62
- Frozen Chicken Thighs In The Air Fryer .. 62
- Air Fryer Frozen Turkey Burgers 62
- Air-fryer Chicken Wings 63
- Air Fryer Chicken Cordon Bleu 63
- Asian Glazed Crispy Chicken Thighs 64
- Air Fryer Turkey Meatballs 64
- Air Fryer Nashville Hot Chicken Hack 64
- Air Fryer Fried Chicken 65
- Air Fryer Bacon Wrapped Chicken Bites .. 65
- Air Fryer Turkey Breast 66
- Air Fryer Tandoori Turkey Breast 66
- Butter Chicken 66
- Air Fryer Chicken Tenders With Flour 67
- Air Fryer Chicken Nuggets 68
- Chicken Parmesan 68
- Air Fryer Chicken Fried Steak 69
- Air Fryer Chicken Wings 70
- Air Fryer Crumbed Chicken Schnitzel 71
- Air Fryer Chili Crisp Chicken Wings 71
- Crispy Air Fryer Fried Chicken Breast 72
- Air Fryer Doritos Crusted Chicken Strips . 72
- Air Fryer Southwest Chicken 73
- Frozen Chicken Cordon Bleu 73
- Air Fryer Bbq Chicken Thighs 74
- Homemade Air Fryer Chicken Nuggets 74
- Air Fryer Chicken Thighs 74
- Air Fryer Turkey Legs 75
- Air Fryer Buffalo Wings 76

VEGETABLE & & VEGETARIAN RECIPES ... 77

- Air Fryer Brussels Sprouts 77
- Hot Cauliflower Wings 77
- Air Fryer Baked Potato 78
- Smashed Potatoes 79
- Ginger And Soy Salmon Fillets 79
- Air Fryer Potato Gratin 80
- Air Fryer Fried Green Tomatoes 80
- Keto Fried Pickles 80
- Air Fryer Broccoli And Cauliflower 81
- Air Fryer Squash Soup 81
- Air Fryer Herbed Brussels Sprouts 82
- Air Fryer Cauliflower Recipe 82
- Air Fryer Broccoli 82
- Air Fryer Zucchini 82
- Air Fryer Pickles 83
- Air Fryer Vegetarian Pumpkin Schnitzel .. 83
- Air Fryer Cauliflower 84
- Air Fryer Twice-baked Potatoes 84
- Air Fryer Stuffed Peppers 84
- Cajun Prawns With Potato & Corn 85
- Crispy Air Fryer Brussels Sprouts 85
- Air Fryer Fried Pickles 86
- Air Fryer Vegetables 86
- Air Fryer Corn On The Cob 86

SALADS & SIDE DISHES RECIPES ... 87

- Cardamom Roasted Beetroot Salad 87
- Air Fryer Roasted Butternut Salad 87
- Air Fryer Pigs In A Blanket 88
- Air Fryer Asparagus Salad 88
- Crispy Parmesan Potato Wedges 88
- Air Fryer Roasted Garlic 89
- Air Fryer Garlic Knots 89
- Artichoke Wings With Vegan Ranch Dip . 90
- Air Fryer Sweet Potato Casserole 90
- Air Fryer Diced Potatoes 91
- Air Fryer Kielbasa 91

FAVORITE AIR FRYER RECIPES 92

Air Fryer Bratwurst 92
Air Fryer French Bread Pizzas 92
Air Fryer Sausage Rolls 92
Air-fryer White Pizza 93
Air Fryer Frozen Corn Dogs 94
Air Fryer Mini Corn Dogs 94
Char Siu Dinner 94
Air Fryer Flatbread Pizzas 95
Air Fryer Brats 95
Buttermilk Ranch Dressing 95
Air Fryer Cacio E Pepe Spaghetti Squash . 96
Air Fryer Grilled Cheese 96
Air Fryer Fried Brown Rice 97
Air Fryer Totino's Pizza 97
Air Fryer Reheating Leftover Pizza 97
Air Fryer Fried Rice 98
Air Fryer Tostones 98
3 Cheese Air Fryer Mini Pizzas 98
Air Fryer Hot Pockets 98
Air Fryer Jalepeno Poppers 99
Air Fryer Hot Dogs 99
Air Fryer Frozen Mozzarella Sticks 99

SNACKS & APPETIZERS RECIPES 100

Air Fryer Frozen French Fries 100
Curly Fries In The Air Fryer 100
Homemade Chips 100
Frozen Waffle Fries In The Air Fryer 100
Air Fryer Home Fries 101
Air Fryer Green Bean Fries 101
Air Fryer Zucchini Chips 102
Air Fryer French Fries 102
Air Fryer Sweet Potato Cubes 102
Air Fried Cheesy Mashed Potato Balls ... 103
Air Fryer Kale Chips 103
Air Fryer Spicy Onion Rings 103
Air Fryer Beet Chips 104
Air Fryer Popcorn 104
Air Fryer Sweet Potato Fries 105
Air Fryer Nachos 105
Easy Onion Rings 106
Air Fryer Turnip Fries 106
Air-fryer Pineapple Chips 106
Air Fryer Potato Skins 106
Air Fryer Chickpeas Recipe 107
Air Fryer Frozen Crinkle Cut Fries 107
Air Fryer Keto Onion Rings Recipe 108

INTRODUCTION

An air fryer is a kitchen appliance that allows you to cook foods with hot air instead of oil. It's like having your mini convection oven on your countertop! Air fryers rapidly circulate hot air around the food inside the basket or tray. This creates a crispy exterior while locking in moisture and flavor inside. Unlike deep frying or baking in oil, there's no need for excess oils or fats when using an air fryer, making it a healthier cooking option overall. Using my air fryer has become second nature now that I understand its functionality. With adjustable temperature controls and various settings, including pre-programmed modes for specific foods like chicken wings or French fries – cooking with my air fryer feels effortless and foolproof. Plus, it cooks frozen foods well, and fresh veggies are given a new life thanks to this nifty appliance!

BENEFITS OF USING AN AIR FRYER FOR COOKING CANNED FOODS

HEALTHIER COOKING METHOD

I love using my air fryer for cooking canned foods because it's healthier than deep-frying. Using hot air instead of oil makes the food crispy without adding unnecessary calories and fat. This technique also helps retain more nutrients, making it an excellent option for those who want to eat healthily. I don't have to worry about that greasy feeling after eating fried foods. Air frying canned vegetables like green beans or baked goods like biscuits can be a tasty way to enjoy them without all the added fats from traditional frying methods. For example, when I air fry canned green beans with some seasoning and a touch of oil spray, they come out perfectly crispy on the outside and tender on the inside – just what I'm looking for in a side dish! It's amazing how such simple changes can make our meals healthier while tasting delicious. Overall, using an air fryer as an alternative cooking method is perfect for those who want to cut back on oily or fatty foods but still enjoy satisfying snacks and meals. Learning how to cook canned foods in my air fryer has been fun and rewarding as someone who loves experimenting with different recipes and ingredients.

TIME-SAVING

Using an air fryer to cook canned foods is not only healthier but also a time-saving method.
You can have your favorite canned foods cooked in just minutes with the right temperature and timing settings. Compared to traditional cooking methods such as baking or frying, an air fryer reduces cooking time by about 20-30%. It saves cooking time, and cleanup is faster and easier with an air fryer. Unlike conventional ovens or stovetops that require multiple pots and pans, air fryers typically have one removable basket that's easy to clean. Plus, they don't produce much smoke or odor during cooking, making them ideal for quick meals on busy days.

VERSATILITY IN COOKING DIFFERENT TYPES OF CANNED FOODS

One of the most significant benefits of air frying canned foods is its versatility in cooking different canned foods. You can cook almost anything in a can using an air fryer, from vegetables and meats to baked goods, seafood, snacks, and appetizers. For example, canned green beans are a popular vegetable easily cooked in an air fryer for a healthier alternative to traditional fried green beans.
And if you're looking for something more substantial, try making honey-barbecue chicken wings or spicy tuna cakes using your air fryer. The possibilities are endless when it comes to cooking canned foods in an air fryer. With so many options available, knowing which canned foods work best for air frying and how to prepare them properly before placing them inside the appliance is essential.
With these tips and tricks under your belt, you'll be on your way to creating delicious meals with ease!

REDUCED OIL USAGE

One of the most significant benefits of cooking canned foods in an air fryer is the reduced use of oil. Unlike traditional frying methods, you only need a fraction of the oil to achieve crispy and delicious results. This makes it a healthier alternative for those conscious of their calorie intake.

With less oil usage, air frying also minimizes the risk of ingesting harmful substances in heated oils. Compared to deep-frying or sautéing, air frying allows you to cook your favorite canned foods with minimal added fats without compromising taste and texture. By choosing the suitable types of canned foods and coating them lightly with seasoning or batter, you'll have a guilt-free pleasure that will satisfy your cravings without sacrificing your health goals.

CHOOSING THE BEST CANNED FOODS FOR AIR FRYING

When choosing canned foods to air fry, consider the types of vegetables, meats, baked goods, seafood, and snacks that can be fried with reduced oil usage and increased crispiness.

VEGETABLES---I love air frying vegetables because they are healthier and deliver crispy and delicious results. My favorite canned vegetables to cook in the air fryer are green beans and corn, but you can use almost any vegetable you have on hand. Just remember to drain excess liquid before coating them with seasoning or batter. One crucial tip for air frying veggies is not to overcrowd the basket. This ensures that each piece gets evenly cooked and crispy. I also recommend setting the temperature between 375-400°F and cooking for 8-12 minutes, depending on your desired level of crispiness. And if you want an added flavor, try tossing your veggies in a bit of melted butter or oil mixed with herbs or spices before adding them to the basket!

MEATS---Meats can be a delicious addition to your air fryer repertoire. Some great canned meat options include chicken, beef, and pork. Before cooking, drain any excess liquid from the can and pat dry with paper towels. When preparing canned meats for air frying, you can coat them in various seasonings or batter for added flavor and texture. Remember that wet batter should be avoided as it will not cook evenly in the air fryer. Instead, use a dry coating or spices like paprika or garlic powder.

By following these tips and experimenting with different recipes, you'll soon discover how versatile your air fryer can be when cooking canned meats!

BAKED GOODS---Baked goods are a delicious addition to any meal and can be made even better using an air fryer.Canned biscuits, cinnamon rolls, and gingerbread bites are just a few examples of baked goods that can be made in the air fryer. The reduced oil usage makes them healthier and creates a crispy outer layer. When preparing canned baked goods for air frying, it's important to coat them with seasoning or batter before cooking. This will help enhance their flavor and create an even crispier texture.Wet batter foods should not be placed in the air fryer since they tend to cook unevenly, while corn dogs should be pre-fried before being air fried for best results. Following these tips and tricks, you can enjoy perfectly cooked canned baked goods straight from your trusty air fryer!

SEAFOOD---I love cooking seafood in my air fryer. It's a healthier alternative to deep frying and cooks the fish to a perfect crisp. My favorite canned seafood to air fry include shrimp, crab cakes, and even tuna patties. Before you air fry your seafood, drain any excess liquid from the can and season it with your preferred spices or batter for extra flavor. Set your air fryer temperature between 350-400 degrees Fahrenheit, depending on the type of fish you're cooking, and cook them for about 5-8 minutes per side until they are crispy on the outside and tender on the inside. Remember not to overcrowd your air fryer basket, which can cause uneven cooking or lead to food sticking together. With these simple tips, you'll be able to enjoy perfectly cooked canned seafood every time!

SNACKS AND APPETIZERS---Don't forget about snacks and appetizers when it comes to air-frying canned foods. Air fryers can create deliciously crispy and healthier versions of favorite crunchy snacks like popcorn or kale chips. For a heartier snack or party appetizer, try air-frying frozen meatballs or chicken wings for a quick cook time and crispy texture. Remember that wet batter foods should be avoided in the air fryer, but a light coating of seasoning or breadcrumbs can add extra flavor to your snack creations. Another great option for snacking is air-fried sweet potato fries. Sweet potatoes are an excellent source of vitamins A and C and are perfect for those seeking a healthier alternative to traditional french fries. Slice the sweet potatoes into thin strips, coat them with oil and seasoning, then pop them into the air fryer until crispy and tender. With these tasty options, your next game-day spread will be a hit!

PREPARING CANNED FOODS FOR AIR FRYING

Before air frying canned foods, it's essential to drain excess liquid from them and coat them with seasoning or batter for added flavor and texture.

Draining Excess Liquid

When preparing canned foods for air frying, one essential step is draining excess liquid. This is because too much liquid can cause steam, making your food come out soggy instead of crispy.

Ensure you use a strainer or colander to drain any excess water while shaking it well to prevent dripping. For best results, it's recommended that you pat dry the canned foods with paper towels after draining off any liquids. Doing this helps remove more moisture from the food and provides a dry surface for seasoning or coating with batter. By draining excess liquid before cooking, your air-fried canned foods will come out deliciously crispy and perfectly cooked inside!

Coating With Seasoning Or Batter

When it comes to air frying canned foods, adding seasoning or batter can make a world of difference in taste and texture. Try coating vegetables like green beans or sliced potatoes with breadcrumbs mixed with your favorite spices for crispy results. Mix cinnamon and sugar and dredge slices of canned pineapple before placing them in the air fryer for a sweeter option. However, it's important to note that wet batter should not be used when cooking canned foods in an air fryer. The high heat from the appliance will cause the batter to blow around inside the basket and cook unevenly. Instead, opt for dry coatings like panko breadcrumbs or crushed cornflakes for that perfect crunch without making a mess.

Setting Up Your Air Fryer For Cooking Canned Foods

To ensure your canned foods are cooked to perfection in your air fryer, it's vital to set up the appliance correctly – this includes selecting the right temperature and time settings and preheating the basket. Read on for more tips and tricks on making the most out of your air fryer when cooking canned foods!

Temperature And Time Settings

When it comes to air frying canned foods, setting the right temperature and time is crucial for a successful outcome. It's always best to refer to the manual that came with your air fryer for guidance. Generally, most air fryers have a temperature range between 200-400°F, and cooking times can vary between 5-25 minutes depending on your cooking. Preheating your air fryer beforehand is also essential, ensuring even cooking and better results. Once preheated, adjust the temperature settings and watch the food cook. It's always helpful to shake or flip your food halfway through cooking time for an evenly cooked result. Remember, every dish has unique temperature requirements, so consult recipe instructions before starting.

Preheating The Air Fryer
Preheating your air fryer ensures that your canned foods cook evenly and crisp. To preheat your air fryer, set the temperature to the recommended level and allow it to heat up for a few minutes before adding your food. It's important not to overcrowd the basket during this process as it can affect the cooking time. Once preheated, place your canned foods in the basket and set the timer according to the recipe or instructions on the packaging. Remember to check on your food halfway through cooking, using tongs or a spatula to flip them over for even cooking. By taking these steps and following our helpful tips, you'll be able to achieve deliciously crispy canned foods cooked in an air fryer every time!

CLEANING YOUR AIR FRYER PROPERLY

Cleaning your air fryer properly is crucial to maintaining its efficiency and prolonging lifespan.
This includes removing excess grease and food debris, wiping down the interior and exterior of the appliance, as well as checking and replacing the air filter regularly.

Removing excess grease and food debris
I always make sure to clean my air fryer properly after each use. To remove excess grease and food debris, I use a damp cloth or sponge to wipe down the exterior and interior of the appliance. It's important to be gentle while cleaning to not damage the non-stick coating. Another helpful tip is removing leftover crumbs or debris from the bottom of the basket using a kitchen brush or toothbrush. Add dish soap and water to your cloth or sponge for extra cleaning power if there are stubborn stains. Keeping your air fryer clean and free from buildup will perform better and last longer overall.

Wiping Down the Interior And Exterior Of The Air Fryer
Keeping your air fryer clean is essential to prevent buildup and ensure optimal performance. Wiping down the interior and exterior of the air fryer is crucial in maintaining its longevity. After each use, allow the appliance to cool before unplugging it and wiping down the inside with a damp cloth. To clean the exterior of your air fryer, wipe it down with a damp cloth or sponge. Avoid using harsh chemicals or abrasive materials that could damage the surface. Regular cleaning will keep your appliance looking new and prevent any unwanted odors from forming while cooking different types of foods. Remember to also check and replace your air filter regularly per manufacturer instructions. This ensures that airflow remains consistent during cooking, resulting in evenly cooked food every time you prepare something delicious in your beloved air fryer!

Checking And Replacing The Air Filter Regularly
A critical aspect of maintaining your air fryer is regularly checking and replacing the air filter. The air filter ensures that your appliance operates properly by preventing dust and other particles from entering the heating element. Over time, the air filter can become dirty, clogged, or damaged, affecting its ability to trap debris effectively. To check the condition of your air filter, gently remove it from its slot at the back of the unit. If you notice any signs of damage or excessive buildup on the filter, it's time to replace it with a new one. Most manufacturers recommend replacing your air filter every three months for optimal performance and longevity of your appliance. By checking and replacing your air filters regularly, you'll enjoy better-tasting foods cooked in a cleaner environment while extending the lifespan of your valuable kitchen gadget.

AIR FRYERS FREQUENTLY ASKED QUESTIONS

Can I put oil in an air fryer? ----- Most recipes only call for about 1 tablespoon of oil, which is best applied with a mister. Fatty foods, like bacon, won't need you to add any oil. Leaner meats, however, will need some oiling to keep them from sticking to the pan.

What shouldn't you put in an Air Fryer? ----- The Air Fryer is one of those kitchen inventions that seem too good to be true. You can cook practically any food in the hot air multi-cooker. However, there are mistakes a lot of us do when handling an air fryer including not preheating your air fryer, not giving the air fryer enough space, overcrowding the air fryer basket, using too little oil, cutting vegetables too small, using wet batters and not washing the air fryer often enough.

Can I use Aluminum Foil or Baking Paper in the Air Fryer? ----- As a general rule, you can use both on the bottom of the air fryer if the basket sits on top. Using aluminum foil or baking paper in the basket technically can be done as long as it's weighed down by the food however it's not recommended because an air fryer works by providing a constant air flow around the cooking cavity.

Should I shake the basket while cooking? ----- Yes, shaking is allowed. A number of foods will stick to the basket if you don't shake it while cooking. Giving it a little shake is specially helpful if you overlap foods, this way the contents of the basket will cook evenly.

What's the first thing I should cook in my new Air Fryer? ----- The most common foods to start with are French Fries, and also Chicken Drumsticks.

What are the disadvantages to cooking in an Air Fryer? ----- The only real disadvantage to cooking in an air fryer is the fact most of the air fryers on the market have small cooking cavities.

What kind of foods can you cook in an Air Fryer? ----The air fryer is your ticket to healthier fried foods that still taste crispy-crunchy delicious and leaves you with a lot less mess at clean-up time. Whether frozen food or raw meat or reheating leftover food, the hot air multi-cooker does a fantastic job. Having an air fryer means you can go ahead and cook frozen food such as frozen fries, nuggets, fish sticks etc. You can also cook raw meat, for example you can roast chicken or pork in the fryer. And you can certainly roast vegetables and nuts too.

Should I pause the Air Fryer when checking on the food? ----- Since you generally only spend a matter of seconds checking, or shaking the food, it is not necessary to pause the air fryer.

Can I open the Air Fryer while cooking? ----- Every Air Fryer is slightly different however going on the premise that heat rises, if your air fryer opens by sliding a basket out from the side or front, then there should be no reason why you can't open the basket for short periods of time.

Should I preheat the Air Fryer? ----- Every Air Fryer manufacturer will have their own recommendations for their particular air fryer. This is also a good idea since many users find that cooking times are more accurate if you preheat first.

Why are my cooking times different? ----- Not all Air Fryers are created equal. Air Fryers work by circulating hot air around the food. The internal shape of the Air Fryer and how the air flows, as well as how hot the air is all contribute to how long it takes to cook a food. This is why you should check often and only use temperatures as a guide until you know how your particular Air Fryer cooks.

What are the advantages to cooking in an Air Fryer? ----- Advantages are many, like we said before, we're talking about a healthier form of cooking. Even though your food is fried it won't be dripping with oil. It's less expensive to run. Cooking in an air fryer is very quick. Also, food cooked in an air fryer is generally really tasty simply because the food is crispy on the outside, and juicy and tender on the inside.

DESSERTS RECIPES

Roasted Pears & Shortbread
Servings: 6

Ingredients:
- For the shortbread
- 65g unsalted butter, room temperature
- 30g light brown soft or light muscovado sugar
- 75g plain flour
- 15g cornflour
- Pinch fine sea salt
- For the roasted pears
- 6 (approx. 150g each) conference pears
- 2 small lemons
- 1 small orange
- 80ml honey
- 15g unsalted butter
- 2 tbsp water
- To serve crème fraîche

Directions:
1. Cream the butter, sugar and salt together in a bowl for about one minute. Combine the plain flour and cornflour together well before adding to the creamed mixture and mixing to bring together. Chill
2. before using
3. Pat the mixture out onto a piece of baking parchment to a rectangle shape 16cm by 12cm. Place on a tray and chill for for 20-30 minutes, or until firm
4. Squeeze one of the lemons into a bowl and add enough cold water to eventually cover the pears. Peel the pears and place into the bowl as you go. With a peeler, peel 3-4 strips on both the remaining lemon and orange. Squeeze both and add the juice to a small saucepan along with the peel, honey, butter and 2 tablespoons of water. Heat to just dissolve the butter
5. When the shortbread dough is firm, prick all over with a fork and cut into 6 rough squares
6. Remove the crisper plates from both drawers. Arrange the pears lying down in the Zone 1 drawer. Pour all the juice and honey mixture over them then insert drawer in unit. Place the 6 shortbread biscuits in Zone 2 drawer, making sure to leave space around them then insert drawer in unit. There is no need to grease the drawer as the buttery biscuits won't stick!
7. Select Zone 1, turn the dial to select ROAST, set temperature to 190°C and set time to 40 minutes. Select Zone 2, turn the dial to select BAKE, set temperature to 150°C and set time to 35 minutes. Press the dial to begin cooking
8. Carefully give the pears a turn and baste 2 to 3 times whilst they are cooking. Check that they are tender with a knife or you can roast them for longer
9. Remove the shortbread from the drawer with help of a small plastic spatula and place them on a rack to cool. The cooking juices can be reduced in a saucepan to desired consistency if necessary. Serve the pears and shortbread with crème fraîche

Cranberry Orange Sweet Rolls

Ingredients:
- (dough ingredients)
- 3 1/2 cups all purpose flour
- 2 1/4 tsp instant dry yeast
- Zest of one orange
- 1/3 cup butter
- 1/3 cup sugar
- 3/4 tsp salt
- 1 1/4 cups milk
- 1 egg
- (filing ingredients)
- 2 cups fresh cranberries, whole and chopped
- 1/2 cup granulated sugar
- zest and juice of one orange
- 1/4 cup butter melted (use 1/3 cup cranberry jelly in place of the butter, if desired)
- 1-2 tsp olive oil for rolling out dough
- Butter for greasing the pan
- (glaze ingredients)
- 3 tablespoons orange juice

- 1 cup powdered sugar

Directions:
1. In a large bowl, mix the all purpose flour and the yeast. Add the orange zest into the flour mixture.
2. Next, melt 1/3 cup butter in a saucepan over medium heat. Once it's melted and starts to bubble, turn off the heat and stir in the sugar and the salt until the grains begin to dissolve in the hot butter. Add the milk slowly, stirring constantly. Once it feels only slightly warm to the touch (slightly above room temperature) you're good to add in the egg and whisk it into the mixture.
3. Pour the wet ingredients into the dry ingredients.
4. Using the dough hooks, mix on low and watch the ingredients combine. After about a minute you should see a sticky dough starting to come together. If you need to turn the mixer off and scrape down the sides and bottom of the bowl, you can.
5. Turn up the mixer speed slightly and allow the mixture to knead the dough for about 3 minutes. The dough should be tacky to the touch, but not so sticky that it's very messy. It should pull away from the sides of the bowl easily. If the dough appears too sticky, continue kneading and add flour, one tablespoon at a time, until the dough reaches that tacky texture.
6. Cover the bowl with some plastic wrap and move it to a warm place in your kitchen to rise for about 1 1/2 to 2 hours.
7. To make the filling: add the chopped and whole cranberries to a large bowl and stir them together with the sugar, orange zest and orange juice.
8. After the dough has risen fully, turn the dough out onto a work surface that's been very lightly greased with vegetable oil. Using a rolling pin, roll out the dough evenly until you have a rectangle shape. Brush the dough with the melted butter (or cranberry jelly, if using this instead).
9. Spread the cranberry mixture evenly over the rectangle of dough.
10. Roll up the dough from the long side until you've got one long roll. Cut the roll at an even thickness as this promotes even baking.
11. Grease baking pan with some butter. Arrange the pieces in the pan you've greased. An arrangement of about 7-8 rolls.
12. Preheat the Air Fryer Oven to 350°F.
13. Once the oven has preheated, bake for about 25-30 minutes, or until they're a nice even light golden brown color.
14. Remove the pan from the oven and let them cool on the pan for about 20-25 minutes.
15. While the buns are cooling, begin making the glaze by mixing together the powdered sugar and orange juice, just until a drizzle-consistency is reached.
16. Drizzle the glaze over the buns when they're cooled almost completely.
17. Sprinkle some additional cranberries and orange zest over the top, and serve!

Air-fryer Chocolate Swirl Meringues
Servings: 4
Cooking Time: 20 Minutes

Ingredients:
- 2 eggs, white only
- 1/2 cup caster sugar
- pinch cream of tartar
- 1/2 tsp white vinegar
- 1/2 tsp cornflour
- 2 tsp Dutch cocoa powder, sifted
- 1 cup thickened cream, whipped
- 125g strawberries, halved

Directions:
1. Using an electric mixer, beat egg, sugar and cream of tartar together for 10 minutes or until mixture is thick and glossy and sugar has dissolved. Add vinegar and cornflour. Beat for 20 seconds until combined. Add cocoa. Fold mixture twice to form a rippled effect.
2. Line the basket of a 12-litre air fryer with baking paper. Spoon 4 large spoonfuls of meringue mixture onto baking paper. Set temperature to 120°C. Cook for 20 minutes or until meringues are dry to the touch.

Stand meringues in the air fryer for 1 hour to cool. Serve dolloped with cream and topped with strawberries.

Peppermint Cookies

Ingredients:
- 1/2 cup butter, softened
- 1/4 cup confectioners sugar
- 1/4 tsp peppermint extract
- 1/2 cup + 2 Tbsp flour
- 1/4 cup cornstarch
- 1 cup vanilla frosting, store bought or homemade
- Red food coloring
- Peppermint candies, crushed

Directions:
1. Preheat your air fryer oven to 350°F.
2. In a mixing bowl, add the softened butter, confectioners sugar and peppermint extract and mix. Set aside.
3. In another bowl, whisk together the flour and cornstarch.
4. Next, add in the wet ingredients in with the dry ingredients. This will make a crumbly dough.
5. Refrigerate for about 30 minutes.
6. Grease the air fryer's baking sheet.
7. Remove the dough from the refrigerator and roll into 6 regular sized cookie balls or about 8-10 small cookies.
8. Bake for 10 minutes then cool on a rack for at least 10 minutes.
9. Take your 1 cup of frosting and combine 1-2 drops of red food coloring to make a subtle reddish, pinky color.
10. Put the peppermint candies in a baggy and crush.
11. Frost the tops of each cookie and sprinkle with the crushed peppermint candies!

Air Fried Marshmallow Peeps

Servings: 4
Cooking Time: 5 Minutes

Ingredients:
- 1 package Marshmallow Peeps
- 1 Can Crescent Rolls 8 crescent rolls

Directions:
1. To make these peeps, begin by unrolling and separating each crescent roll.
2. Place one peep at the end of the crescent toll and roll until it is completely wrapped. Be sure to pinch any exposed parts of the peep.
3. Spray basket with nonstick cooking spray, or line with air fryer parchment paper. Place wrapped peeps in the prepared basket, leaving a small space in between peeps.
4. Air fry peeps at 350 degrees for about 5 minutes, until crescent rolls are golden brown
5. Carefully remove them from the Air fryer. Sprinkle with powdered sugar, drizzle with chocolate syrup or frosting glaze.

NOTES
I make these in my Cosori 5.8 air fryer. Depending on size and wattage of the air fryer, you may need to add 1-2 additional minutes to cook time.
Leave enough room in between wrapped peeps, allowing room for the roll puff as it cooks.
Do not stack or overlap peeps in the basket. The dough may not cook evenly.
You can make 4 or 8 fried peeps in a batch, depending on what will fit in your basket.

Easy Air Fryer Donuts

Servings: 10
Cooking Time: 10 Minutes

Ingredients:
- 1 can biscuits
- ¼ cup butter melted
- ½ cup sugar
- 1 tablespoon cinnamon

Directions:
1. Preheat air fryer to 350°F.
2. Cut a circle out of the center of each biscuit using a small 1" cutter.
3. Place 4-5 pieces of the dough in the air fryer.
4. Cook 3 minutes. Flip and cook an additional 2-3 minutes or until browned.
5. Remove from the air fryer and while warm, brush with butter. Combine sugar & cinnamon, toss donuts in sugar mixture.

6. Repeat with remaining donuts. Once the donuts are cooked, add the donut holes to the air fryer and cook for 3 minutes. Toss with additional butter and sugar if desired.

Notes

If you don't have a 1" cutter, the center can be cut using a large pastry tip.

Donuts can be cooled and glazed or dipped in glaze if preferred.

Bratapfe With Vanilla Sauce

Servings: 5

Ingredients:
- 45g sultanas (golden raisins)
- 1 tbsp rum or bourbon
- 1/3 cup walnuts, chopped
- 1 tbsp apple jelly
- 1 tbsp honey
- 1/4 tsp ground cinnamon
- Pinch sea salt
- 5 apples, cored
- 1 1/2 tbsp butter, cut in 5 pieces
- 50g confectioners' sugar
- 1 tbsp milk
- 1 tsp vanilla extract

Directions:
1. Place sultanas and rum into a small microwave-safe bowl. Microwave until liquid simmers, about 30 seconds. Set aside.
2. Insert crisper plate in pan and pan in unit. Preheat unit by selecting ROAST, setting temperature to 160°C and setting time to 5 minutes. Select START/STOP to begin.
3. In a bowl, stir together walnuts, jelly, honey, cinnamon, salt and soaked sultanas. Set aside.
4. Place apples onto a large sheet of aluminum foil, folding up edges to create a bowl.
5. Place foil with apples into the unit. Using a small spoon, stuff walnut filling equally into the center of each apple and top each with a piece of butter. Select ROAST, set temperature to 160°C and set time to 25 minutes. Select START/STOP to begin.
6. While apples are cooking, combine confectioners' sugar, milk and vanilla in a small bowl.
7. After 20 minutes, remove pan from unit. Drizzle confectioners' sugar mixture evenly over each apple. Reinsert pan and select START/STOP to resume cooking.
8. When cooking is complete, remove foil and allow apples to cool briefly. Serve warm, spooning sauce over apples.

Air-fryer Peaches With Vanilla-bean Ricotta

Servings: 4
Cooking Time: 15 Minutes

Ingredients:
- 4 yellow peaches, halved, destoned
- 1 tbs maple syrup
- 1 pinch ground cinnamon
- 1 cup light smooth ricotta
- 1/2 tsp vanilla-bean paste

Directions:
1. Place peaches in an air-fryer basket and brush with half of the maple syrup. Set temperature to 180°C and cook for 10 minutes or until peaches have softened.
2. Sprinkle with half of the cinnamon. Cook for a further 1 minute or until golden and caramelised.
3. Meanwhile, combine ricotta and vanilla in a small bowl.
4. Remove peaches from air fryer and drizzle with remaining maple syrup. Serve dolloped with ricotta mixture and sprinkled with remaining cinnamon.

Air-fryer Hot-cross-bun Ice-cream Balls

Servings: 4
Cooking Time: 10 Minutes

Ingredients:
- 500g vanilla ice-cream
- 1 pkt traditional hot cross buns
- 3 free range eggs
- 2 cups milk
- 5ml extra virgin olive oil cooking spray
- 1 cup caramel fudge topping
- 125g raspberries

- 2 bananas, sliced

Directions:
1. Line a baking tray with baking paper. Scoop ice-cream into 4 large walnut-sized balls. Place on tray and freeze for 2 hours or until very firm.
2. Roughly tear hot cross buns into pieces and then process until fine crumbs form.
3. Place on a large flat plate. Whisk eggs and milk in a large bowl.
4. Working quickly with one ball at a time, using 2 forks to hold ice-cream, dip in egg mixture then roll in hot-cross-bun crumbs to thickly coat, making sure ice-cream is completely covered in a thick layer of crumb. Then repeat to double crumb.
5. Place on tray and freeze for 4 hours or overnight until very firm.
6. Line basket of a 4L air fryer with baking paper. Spray ice-cream balls with cooking oil, then place in the air-fryer basket. Cook for 2-3 minutes on 200°C, or until golden brown and crisp. Carefully transfer balls to serving bowls. Drizzle with topping and serve with raspberries and banana.

St Patrick's Day Air Fryer Oven Chocolate Guinness Cupcakes

Ingredients:
- 2 cups all-purpose flour
- 1 teaspoon baking soda
- 1 teaspoon baking powder
- ¾ teaspoon salt
- 1 cup butter
- 1 cup Guinness stout
- ¾ cup special cocoa powder
- 1 tablespoon instant coffee granules
- 1 ½ cups granulated sugar
- ½ cup packed brown sugar
- 2 teaspoons vanilla
- 3 eggs
- ¾ cup sour cream
- 1 ½ cups butter, softened
- 4 cups powdered sugar
- 6 tablespoons Irish cream liqueur or caramel-flavor coffee creamer
- ⅓ cup caramel sauce
- ½ cup assorted green and/or gold sprinkles

Directions:
1. Line twenty-four 2 1/2-inch muffin cups with cupcake liners. In a large bowl whisk together flour, baking soda, baking powder, and 3/4 teaspoon salt, set aside.
2. In separate bowl, add 1 cup of hot melted butter, add in the room temperature Guinness, cocoa powder, instant coffee, and granulated sugar. Continue stirring until smooth.
3. In the bowl of an electric mixer, or hand held mixer, combine brown sugar and 1 teaspoon of the vanilla. Add melted butter mixture and beat on medium-low until cooled. Add eggs one at a time, beating after each addition until eggs are incorporated.
4. With mixer on medium, combine flour and batter mixtures. Once combined, add the sour cream, beating until combined and scraping down the sides of the bowl as necessary. Divide batter evenly among muffin cups. (They will be nearly full.)
5. Bake at 300 F for about 18 to 25 minutes or until a toothpick inserted in the centers comes out clean. Let cool in pans 5 minutes; remove to wire rack. Let cool.
6. Frosting:
7. For frosting: In the bowl of an electric mixer beat the softened butter on medium-high until creamy. Reduce speed; add powdered sugar, liqueur, caramel sauce, and the remaining 1 teaspoon vanilla. Increase speed to medium-high; beat until frosting is smooth and fluffy.
8. Pipe or frost cupcakes and add sprinkles. Makes 24 cupcakes. Enjoy!

How To Make Apple Pie Bombs In Your Air Fryer

Ingredients:
- ¾ cup granulated sugar
- 3 teaspoons apple pie spice
- 1 can (8 count) Pillsbury Grand biscuits
- 1 cup apple pie filling, with apples cut into small pieces
- 1 teaspoon cinnamon

- 1 stick butter, melted

Directions:
1. In a medium-size bowl, mix the sugar and apple pie spice. Set aside.
2. Remove the biscuits from the can and separate each into two layers. Using a rolling pin, roll each layer of biscuit into a 4-inch circle. (until you are left with 16 circles.)
3. In a small bowl, combine the apple pie filling with cinnamon. Mix to combine.
4. Spoon about 1 tablespoon of the apple pie filling and cinnamon mixture into the center of each circle.
5. Use your fingers to pull sides together and pinch to seal. Roll into balls.
6. Spray the basket of an air fryer with nonstick cooking spray.
7. Working in batches, place the balls into an air fryer basket about 2 inches apart. Spray the tops with cooking spray.
8. Air fry at 350°F for 8-9 minutes, or until golden brown.
9. Carefully remove the balls from the air fryer, dipping or brushing each in melted butter.
10. Roll each dipped apple pie bomb into the apple pie spice and sugar mixture. Repeat with the remaining batches.
11. Serve immediately or at room temperature and enjoy!

Air Fryer Homemade Cannoli

Servings: 20

Ingredients:
- FOR THE FILLING:
- 1 (16-oz.) container ricotta
- 1/2 c. mascarpone cheese
- 1/2 c. powdered sugar, divided
- 3/4 c. heavy cream
- 1 tsp. pure vanilla extract
- 1 tsp. orange zest
- 1/4 tsp. kosher salt
- 1/2 c. mini chocolate chips, for garnish
- FOR THE SHELLS:
- 2 c. all-purpose flour, plus more for surface
- 1/4 c. granulated sugar
- 1 tsp. kosher salt
- 1/2 tsp. cinnamon
- 4 tbsp. cold butter, cut into cubes
- 6 tbsp. white wine
- 1 large egg
- 1 egg white, for brushing
- Vegetable oil, for frying
- See All Nutritional Information

Directions:
1. MAKE FILLING:
2. Drain ricotta by placing it a fine mesh strainer set over a large bowl. Let drain in refrigerator for at least an hour and up to overnight.
3. In a large bowl using a hand mixer, beat heavy cream and 1/4 cup powdered sugar until stiff peaks form.
4. In another large bowl, combine ricotta, mascarpone, remaining 1/4 cup powdered sugar, vanilla, orange zest, and salt. Fold in whipped cream. Refrigerate until ready to fill cannoli, at least 1 hour.
5. MAKE SHELLS:
6. In a large bowl, whisk together flour, sugar, salt, and cinnamon. Cut butter into flour mixture with your hands or pastry cutter until pea-sized. Add wine and egg and mix until a dough forms. Knead a few times in bowl to help dough come together. Pat into a flat circle, then wrap in plastic wrap and refrigerate at least 1 hour and up to overnight.
7. On a lightly floured surface, divide dough in half. Roll one half out to ⅛" thick. Use a 4" circle cookie cutter to cut out dough. Repeat with remaining dough. Re-roll scraps to cut a few extra circles.
8. Wrap dough around cannoli molds and brush egg whites where the dough will meet to seal together.
9. FOR FRYING:
10. In a large pot over medium heat, heat about 2" of oil to 360°. Working in batches, add cannoli molds to oil and fry, turning occasionally, until golden, about 4 minutes. Remove from oil and place on a paper towel-lined plate. Let cool slightly.

11. When cool enough to handle or using a kitchen towel to hold, gently twist shells off of molds to remove.
12. Place filling in a pastry bag fitted with an open star tip. Pipe filling into shells, then dip ends in mini chocolate chips.
13. FOR AIR FRYER:
14. Working in batches, place molds in basket of air fryer and cook at 350° for 12 minutes, or until golden.
15. When cool enough to handle or using a kitchen towel to hold, gently remove twist shells off of molds.
16. Place filling in a pastry bag fitted with an open star tip. Pipe filling into shells, then dip ends in mini chocolate chips.

Maple Roasted Acorn Squash
Servings: 4
Cooking Time: 15 Minutes

Ingredients:
- 1 acorn squash
- 1 tablespoon olive oil
- 2 tablespoons maple syrup
- 1/8 teaspoon coarse sea salt

Directions:
1. Preheat oven to 375 degrees (see below for air fryer directions).
2. Cut acorn squash in half and scoop out pulp and seeds.
3. Cut halves into 1-inch slices.
4. Spread oil on both side of slices and place on a baking sheet in a single even layer.
5. Baste maple syrup on top of each acorn squash slice.
6. Sprinkle sea salt on top evenly.
7. Bake for 15-20 minutes until fork pierces it easily.
8. Enjoy immediately or keep refrigerated for up to 3 days reheating prior to serving.

NOTES
*Air Fryer Directions:
Prepare acorn squash as stated above.
Place slices in air fryer in a single layer.
Cook at 380 degrees for 10-12 minutes until easily pierced with a fork.

Lemon Meringue Cupcakes
Servings: 4
Cooking Time: 12 Minutes

Ingredients:
- 1 1/4 cup flour
- 1 tsp baking powder
- A pinch of salt
- 1/2 cup unsalted butter, room temperature
- 3/4 cup sugar
- 2 eggs
- 2 tsp lemon zest
- 1/2 cup milk
- 4 tbsp store bought lemon curd
- Meringue topping:
- 2 egg whites, room temperature
- 4 tbsp fine white sugar

Directions:
1. Set the air fryer to bake and preheat the air fryer to 180 degrees c.
2. In one bowl, cream the butter and sugar together.
3. Add the eggs and mix until combined.
4. Add the flour, baking powder, lemon zest and salt to the egg mixture and mix well.
5. Place the silicone muffin moulds in the air fryer and fill them with the mixture.
6. Set the timer to 12 minutes and air fry until golden and until a toothpick comes out clean.
7. Remove and allow to cool.
8. To make the meringue icing beat the egg whites until frothy and slowly add the sugar then beat further until the mixture forms stiff peaks.
9. Remove the middle of the cupcake with a small spoon and set aside.
10. Fill the cupcake with lemon curd.
11. Pipe the meringue mixture on the cupcake and put the cupcakes back in the air fryer for 38 seconds to get the golden top.

Air Fryer Oreo

Servings: 4
Cooking Time: 5 Minutes

Ingredients:
- 8 Oreos or other sandwich cookies
- 1 package Pillsbury Crescents Rolls (or crescent dough sheet)
- Powdered sugar for dusting (optional)

Directions:
1. Spread out crescent dough onto a cutting board or counter.
2. Using your finger, press down into each perforated line so it forms one big sheet. Cut into eighths.
3. Place an Oreo cookie in the center of each of the crescent roll squares and roll each corner up.
4. Bunch up the rest of the crescent roll to make sure it covers the entire Oreo cookie. Do not stretch the crescent roll too thin or it will break.
5. Preheat your air fryer to 320 degrees.
6. Gently place the Air Fried Oreos inside the air fryer in one even row so they do not touch.
7. Cook Oreos for 5-6 minutes until golden brown on the outside.
8. Carefully remove the Air Fryer Oreos from the air fryer and immediately dust them with powdered sugar if desired.

Air-fryer Apple Fritters

Servings: 15
Cooking Time: 10 Minutes

Ingredients:
- 1-1/2 cups all-purpose flour
- 1/4 cup sugar
- 2 teaspoons baking powder
- 1-1/2 teaspoons ground cinnamon
- 1/2 teaspoon salt
- 2/3 cup 2% milk
- 2 large eggs, room temperature
- 1 tablespoon lemon juice
- 1-1/2 teaspoons vanilla extract, divided
- 2 medium Honeycrisp apples, peeled and chopped
- Cooking spray
- BROWNED BUTTER GLAZE:
- 1/4 cup butter
- 1 cup confectioners' sugar
- 1 tablespoon 2% milk

Directions:
1. Preheat air fryer to 410°. In a large bowl, combine flour, sugar, baking powder, cinnamon and salt. Add milk, eggs, lemon juice and 1 teaspoon vanilla extract; stir just until moistened. Fold in apples.
2. Line air-fryer basket with parchment (cut to fit); spritz with cooking spray. In batches, drop dough by 1/4 cupfuls 2 in. apart onto parchment. Spritz with cooking spray. Cook until golden brown, 5-6 minutes. Turn fritters; continue to air-fry until golden brown, 1-2 minutes.
3. Melt butter in small saucepan over medium-high heat. Carefully cook until butter starts to brown and foam, about 5 minutes. Remove from heat; cool slightly. Add confectioners' sugar, 1 tablespoon milk and remaining 1/2 teaspoon vanilla extract to browned butter; whisk until smooth. Drizzle over fritters before serving.

Cinnamon Apple Oatmeal Dog Treats

Servings: 40
Cooking Time: 4 Hours

Ingredients:
- 2½ cups quick-cook oats, divided
- 1 cup applesauce (only ingredient should be apples)
- ½ teaspoon cinnamon
- 2 eggs, lightly beaten
- Items Needed
- Food processor or blender

Directions:
1. Place 2 cups of the quick-cook oats in a food processor or blender and pulse until it resembles a coarse flour. Place in a large mixing bowl.
2. Add the remaining oats, applesauce, cinnamon, and eggs and mix until well combined and forms a dough.

3. Divide the mixture into roughly ½-tablespoon-sized portions and place them evenly between the Food Dehydrator trays.
4. Set temperature to 135°F and time to 4 hours, then press Start/Stop.
5. Remove the treats when done and dried but not crispy. Cool completely, then serve to your pet.

Air Fryer Grilled Cheese

Servings: 2
Cooking Time: 5 Minutes

Ingredients:
- 4 slices sandwich bread or sourdough bread
- 4 ounces sharp cheddar
- 2 tablespoons butter

Directions:
1. Preheat the air fryer to 350°F.
2. Butter one side of each slice of bread. Place the cheese between two slices of bread, with the buttered side facing out.
3. Place the sandwiches in the air fryer basket in a single layer.
4. Cook for 4-6 minutes, or until the bread is golden brown and the cheese is melted.

Notes

Tip: If the bread (or cheese) is thin or light, it might blow off the sandwich while cooking. To ensure your sandwich stays together, use thicker bread and cheese, or lightly butter both sides of the bread. You may also secure it with toothpicks.

Cooking time: Air fryers can vary, you may need to cook your sandwiches for a minute more or less.

Variations: Swap out the cheddar for any cheese you have on hand. A pinch of garlic powder can be added to the outside of the bread. Add in your favorites. Bacon, tomato slices, jalapenos, the possibilities are endless.

Cherry Hand Pies

Servings: 14
Cooking Time: 8 Minutes

Ingredients:
- Cherry Hand Pie:
- 12 ounces frozen or fresh cherries, pitted
- 1 tablespoon lemon juice
- ¼ cup granulated sugar
- A pinch of kosher salt
- 1 tablespoon cornstarch
- ½ teaspoon almond extract
- 2 sheets frozen puff pastry, thawed
- 1 egg, beaten
- Glaze:
- 1 cup powdered sugar
- 1 tablespoon whole milk
- ½ teaspoon vanilla extract
- Items Needed:
- Rolling pin
- 3-inch round cutter
- Baking sheet
- Wax paper

Directions:
1. Combine the cherries, lemon juice, sugar, and salt in a saucepan over medium-high heat. Bring mixture to a boil, then reduce to a simmer for 5 minutes.
2. Smash some of the cherries lightly with a fork.
3. Place the cornstarch in a small bowl. Add 3 tablespoons of the cherry liquid and stir until no clumps remain.
4. Pour the cornstarch mixture into the saucepan and stir. When the mixture thickens, remove from heat, stir in the almond extract, and refrigerate until slightly chilled.
5. Roll out each puff pastry sheet on a floured surface into a 9 x 12-inch rectangle. Using a 3-inch round cutter, cut out circles in the puff pastry.
6. Place the circles onto a baking sheet lined with wax paper.
7. Spoon about 2 teaspoons of cherry filling onto half of the puff pastry circles. Brush the edges with some of the beaten egg and place the remaining puff pastry circles on top to enclose.

8. Press the edges with a fork to seal. Refrigerate for 20 minutes.
9. Select the Preheat function on the Air Fryer, adjust temperature to 350°F, and press Start/Pause.
10. Cut a 1-inch vent in the top of each pastry. Brush the tops with more of the beaten egg.
11. Place the cherry hand pies into the preheated fryer baskets.
12. Set time to 8 minutes, then press Start/Pause.
13. Remove when golden and puffed. Transfer to a wire rack immediately and allow to cool completely.
14. Whisk the glaze ingredients together in a small bowl until smooth, then glaze the cooled cherry hand pies.
15. Serve the pies when the glaze is set.

Shrunken Apple Punch

Ingredients:
- 6 medium apples
- 1 gallon apple cider
- 4 cinnamon sticks
- 2 lemons
- 2 cups spiced rum/cinnamon whiskey (optional)
- Whole cloves

Directions:
1. Peel the apples and cut in half lengthwise. Scoop out the seeds and core.
2. Carve faces into the rounded side of the apple. Spritz with lemon juice to keep fresh.
3. Place apples face side up in the prepared sheet pan. Press cloves into the eye socket.
4. Bake at 250 for an hour or until the faces start to brown and dehydrate.
5. In a pressure cooker (or on stove top) add apple cider and keep warm.
6. When ready to serve, add the shrunken skulls to the cider.
7. Serve warm with 1 shrunken head.

Air Fryer Bananas
Servings: 2

Ingredients:
- 2 ripe bananas
- 1 tablespoon coconut oil, melted
- 1 teaspoon coconut sugar (or brown sugar)
- 1/4 teaspoon ground cinnamon

Directions:
1. Peel your bananas and lay them on a cutting board. Cut each banana in half and then cut each halved section down the middle lengthwise.
2. Place your peeled and halved bananas into a bowl.
3. Then, in a small bowl, combine the coconut oil, coconut sugar, and cinnamon. Stir gently to combine.
4. Add the melted coconut oil, sugar, and cinnamon to the bananas. Gently toss to combine. You can also use a pastry brush to coat the bananas with the mixture as opposed to tossing them, if you prefer.
5. Lay a piece of aluminum foil or parchment paper in the bottom of your air fryer basket. Poke a few holes in the foil or paper to help the hot air circulate.
6. Place your coated banana halves in a single layer on top of the aluminum foil or paper. Set the time to 375°F for 5 minutes.
7. After the five minutes are up, turn the bananas over and cook them for an additional 2-3 minutes, or until they have started to caramelize and turn a golden brown.
8. Serve warm. These Air Fryer Bananas are great plain or topped with your choice of ice cream or whipped cream.

Notes

You can easily double or triple this recipe depending on how may servings you want to make.

Air fried bananas are best served right after they are done cooking.

If you don't have coconut oil and aren't on a vegan or dairy-free diet, you can also use melted butter or ghee in this recipe.

Halloween Cupcakes In The Air Fryer Oven

Ingredients:

Cupcakes:
- 12 tbsp butter
- 1/2 sugar
- 3 eggs
- 2 1/2 vanilla extract
- 1/2 cup sour cream
- 1 cup buttermilk
- 1 cup melted baking chocolate
- 1 3/4 cup all-purpose flour
- 1 1/2 tsp baking soda
- 1/4 tsp salt

Frosting:
- 12 oz cream cheese
- 1 1/2 tbsp butter
- 1 1/2 cup powdered sugar
- Red and yellow food coloring

Directions:
1. Cake Batter:
2. In a large mixing bowl, add 12 tbsp of butter and 1/2 cup sugar.
3. Beat with a mixer until creamy.
4. Once creamy, beat in three eggs, one at a time.
5. Then, 2 1/2 tsp Vanilla extract and set aside
6. In a medium mixing bowl, whisk together 1/2 cup sour cream and 1 cup buttermilk.
7. In a small mixing bowl, combine 1 cup melted baking chocolate, 1 3/4 all-purpose flour, 1 1/2 tsp baking soda, and 1/4 tsp salt.
8. Now beat together all three ingredients a portion at a time.
9. Fill cupcake wrappers about 2/3 full with the cake batter.
10. Place the cupcakes on the center rack and set the cooking preset to 'Bake' - adjust the temperature to 300° for 5 minutes.
11. After 5 minutes, remove cupcakes, rotate and return to the center rack and bake for another 5 minutes at 300° using the 'Bake' preset.
12. Frosting:
13. In a medium mixing bowl, beat together 12 oz cream cheese, 1 1/2 sticks butter, and 1 1/2 cup of powder sugar.
14. Add in equal portions red and yellow food coloring - mix well.
15. Once the cupcakes are cool, frost each one using a piping bag and have fun decorating!

Vortex Air Fryer Strawberry French Toast Bake

Servings: 8
Cooking Time: 25 Minutes

Ingredients:
- 4 teaspoons butter
- 1 pound loaf of brioche bread
- 8 eggs
- 2 cups milk
- 1 cup heavy cream
- 2 teaspoons vanilla extract
- 1 teaspoon cinnamon
- 8 ounces fresh strawberries cleaned and quartered
- 2 tablespoons brown sugar

Directions:
1. Find a baking dish that will fit in the Vortex. Cut or tear the brioche into chunks and place them in the baking dish.
2. In a large bowl whisk together eggs, milk, cream, vanilla, and cinnamon until well combined
3. Pour egg mixture over the bread, making sure all is coated
4. Cover the dish and cool in fridge overnight
5. Preheat your Air Fryer to 350°F on BAKE.
6. Tuck cut berries into the bread
7. Sprinkle on brown sugar and cover with tin foil
8. Bake for about 20 and then uncover and cook for 5-10 minutes or until golden brown and done in center
9. Serve with powdered sugar and/or syrup if desired

Air Fryer Blueberry Scones

Servings: 16
Cooking Time: 6 Minutes

Ingredients:
- 1/3 cup butter slightly softened
- 1 3/4 cups all purpose flour
- 1/4 cup sugar
- 2 teaspoon baking powder
- 1 large egg
- 3/4 cup fresh or frozen blueberries
- 4 tablespoon milk

Directions:
1. In a medium bowl, combine the butter, flour, sugar, and baking powder. Stir until it become crumbly.
2. Add in the egg, and the milk, one tablespoon at a time, until the dough forms.
3. Stir in the blueberries.
4. Roll the dough, until it is about ½ inch thick. Cut with 2 inch cutter.
5. Place in air fryer basket on parchment paper, or lightly brushed with olive oil.
6. Cook at 380 degrees Fahrenheit for 5-6 minutes, until they are golden.

NOTES
Do not use air fryer with just parchment paper by itself. It must be weighted down by the, or it can be a fire hazard!

Air Fryer Gingersnap Cookies

Servings: 12
Cooking Time: 6 Minutes

Ingredients:
- 1 cup all-purpose flour
- 1/2 cup brown sugar packed
- 1/3 cup butter softened
- 2 tablespoons molasses
- 1 large egg
- 1/2 teaspoon baking soda
- 1/2 teaspoon ground ginger
- Cinnamon Sugar Topping
- 1/4 cup granulated sugar
- 1 tablespoon ground cinnamon

Directions:
1. In a small shallow bowl or flat plate, combine the sugar and cinnamon for the topping. Stir dry ingredients together and set aside.
2. In a medium bowl, cream butter with brown sugar. Add in molasses, egg, baking soda, and ground ginger. Mix on medium speed until mixture becomes thick and creamy.
3. Slowly begin to add in flour (about a ¼ cup at a time). Continue to mix together until a soft dough forms. Make sure all flour from sides of bowl have been fully incorporated into the dough mixture.
4. Use a cookie scoop or spoon shape dough into small balls (about 1-1 ½ inches in size). Roll them in cinnamon sugar mixture and set aside on a baking sheet until all dough has been used.
5. Line your air fryer with parchment paper and place balls in a single layer. Leave enough room between cookies to slightly spread as they cook. Air fry at 320 degrees F for 6-8 minutes.
6. Allow cookies to cool before removing them from your air fryer basket. If you are making a couple of batches, you can remove cookies when slightly warm and let them finish cooling on a wire rack.

NOTES
Optional flavors: Adding a pinch pumpkin pie spice, nutmeg and clove will boost the ginger taste. Creating a family favorite warm spice mixture makes them extra special.
Optional drinks to go with this chewy cookie: Dunking them into a warm cup of tea, a glass of cold milk, a hot toddy or your favorite morning brewed coffee on a cold winter's day are always yummy.

BREAKFAST & BRUNCH RECIPES

Air Fryer Breakfast Sandwiches
Servings: 1
Cooking Time: 10 Minutes

Ingredients:
- 1 Frozen Breakfast Sandwich

Directions:
1. Separate the breakfast sandwich in half. Flip the filling so the cheese lays against the bread (because the cheese will blow off if it is on top). See images in recipe write up above for example.
2. Lay the two halves in the air fryer basket, bread side down/meat & egg side up. Air Fry at 340°F/170°C for 6-8 minutes.
3. Reassemble the breakfast sandwich. Continue to Air Fry at 340°F/170°C for another 2 minutes, or until the bread is golden.

NOTES
Air Frying Tips and Notes:
No Oil Necessary. Cook Frozen - Do not thaw first.
Don't overcrowd the air fryer basket.
Recipe timing is based on a non-preheated air fryer. If cooking in multiple batches of sandwiches back to back, the following batches may cook a little quicker.
Recipes were tested in 3.7 to 6 qt. air fryers. If using a larger air fryer, they might cook quicker so adjust cooking time.

Breakfast Oat Cake
Servings: 1
Cooking Time: 15 Minutes

Ingredients:
- 1/2 banana
- 1/2 cup rolled oats
- 1/3 cup milk of choice
- 1/2 tsp bp
- 1/4 tsp flaked sea salt
- 1T honey
- 1 egg
- 1 square dark chocolate, diced
- 1 Tbsp Cacao (optional for a chocolate cookie cake)
- Vegan Adaption: increase the milk to ⅔ cup, replace the egg with 1Tbsp chia soaked with 2 ½ Tbsp water

Directions:
1. Place the oats, banana, milk, baking powder, salt, oats, and honey in a blender. Blend for 1 minute on high until well combined and the oats are a fine puree.
2. Heat the Instant Vortex to Bake at a temperature of 177C for 13 minutes.
3. Pour the oats into a 250ml ramekin, then place in the preheated Instant Vortex.
4. Once golden brown and cooked through, remove from the Vortex and serve immediately.

Frozen Egg Rolls In The Air Fryer
Servings: 5
Cooking Time: 8 Minutes

Ingredients:
- 5 frozen egg rolls

Directions:
1. Preheat your air fryer to 380 degrees.
2. Place the frozen egg rolls in the air fryer not touching and cook them for 8 to 10 minutes.
3. Remove them from the air fryer, let cool slightly, then enjoy!*
4. *reheat at 350 degrees for 3 minutes, preheated

NOTES
HOW TO COOK FROZEN SPRING ROLLS IN THE AIR FRYER
Preheat your air fryer to 400 degrees.
Place frozen spring rolls in the air fryer and cook for 7 to 8 minutes until warmed thoroughly. Remove from the air fryer and enjoy!*
*reheat at 350 degrees for 2 to 3 minutes, preheated
HOW TO COOK FROZEN MINI EGG ROLLS IN THE AIR FRYER
Preheat your air fryer to 380 degrees.
Place the frozen mini egg rolls in the air fryer and cook for 5 to 7 minutes until warmed thoroughly. Remove them from the air fryer and enjoy!*
*reheat at 350 degrees for about 2 minutes

Air Fryer Bacon And Egg Breakfast Biscuit Bombs

Servings: 10

Ingredients:
- Biscuit Bombs
- 4 slices bacon, cut into 1/2-inch pieces
- 1 tablespoon butter
- 2 eggs, beaten
- 1/4 teaspoon pepper
- 1 can (10.2 oz) refrigerated Pillsbury™ Grands!™ Southern Homestyle Buttermilk Biscuits (5 Count)
- 2 oz sharp cheddar cheese, cut into ten 3/4-inch cubes
- Egg Wash
- 1 egg
- 1 tablespoon water

Directions:
1. Cut two 8-inch rounds of cooking parchment paper. Place one round in bottom of air fryer basket. Spray with cooking spray.
2. In 10-inch nonstick skillet, cook bacon over medium-high heat until crisp. Remove from pan; place on paper towel. Carefully wipe skillet with paper towel. Add butter to skillet; melt over medium heat. Add 2 beaten eggs and pepper to skillet; cook until eggs are thickened but still moist, stirring frequently. Remove from heat; stir in bacon. Cool 5 minutes.
3. Meanwhile, separate dough into 5 biscuits; separate each biscuit into 2 layers. Press each into 4-inch round. Spoon 1 heaping tablespoonful egg mixture onto center of each round. Top with one piece of the cheese. Gently fold edges up and over filling; pinch to seal. In small bowl, beat remaining egg and water. Brush biscuits on all sides with egg wash.
4. Place 5 of the biscuit bombs, seam sides down, on parchment in air fryer basket. Spray both sides of second parchment round with cooking spray. Top biscuit bombs in basket with second parchment round, then top with remaining 5 biscuit bombs.
5. Set to 325°F; cook 8 minutes. Remove top parchment round; using tongs, carefully turn biscuits, and place in basket in single layer. Cook 4 to 6 minutes longer or until cooked through (at least 165°F).

Air Fryer Hash Brown Egg Bites

Servings: 7

Ingredients:
- Deselect All
- Nonstick cooking spray, for the mold
- 4 large eggs
- 1/4 cup heavy cream
- Kosher salt
- 2/3 cup shredded Cheddar
- 1/4 cup diced red bell peppers
- 1 scallion, white and green parts sliced
- 1/2 cup shredded frozen hash browns, thawed

Directions:
1. Special equipment: a 7-cavity silicone egg bites mold, 6-quart air fryer
2. Spray the cavities of a 7-cavity silicone egg bites mold with nonstick spray. Whisk together the eggs, heavy cream and 1/2 teaspoon salt in a large glass measuring cup until no white streaks remain.
3. Divide the egg mixture, 1/3 cup of the Cheddar, the bell peppers and scallions among the cavities of the mold. Gently stir the mixture in each cavity with a spoon. Transfer the mold to the basket of a 6-quart air fryer, set it to 300°F and cook for 3 minutes.
4. Meanwhile, combine the hash browns and remaining 1/3 cup Cheddar in a small bowl. Gently top each egg bite with the hash brown-cheese mixture.
5. Set the air fryer to 300°F and cook for 12 minutes more. The top of each bite should be golden brown and the eggs should be set. Remove the mold and let stand for 10 minutes before popping out the egg bites. Serve warm.

Air Fried Easy Breakfast Pastries
Servings: 4
Cooking Time: 15 Minutes
Ingredients:
- 2 packages refrigerated pie crusts
- A variety of jam, in any flavor you like
- 1 egg, beaten with 1 teaspoon of water
- Icing
- 1/2 cup powdered sugar
- 2-3 tablespoons milk
- Sprinkles

Directions:
1. Roll out the pie dough to about ¼ inch thick. Cut the dough into 6 rectangles about 4" x 6". Spread 2 tablespoons of jam on one side of the rectangle leaving about ½ inch around the edge.
2. Using a pastry brush, coat the edges of the pie dough with egg wash. Add a second pastry rectangle on top and press the edges with a fork. Cut two slits in the top of the dough to vent.
3. Brush the top with egg wash, place on dark-coated, parchment-lined baking sheet.
4. Air Fry at 350°F for 5 minutes, carefully flip the pastries, cook 5 more minutes
5. Carefully move baked pastries to a cooling rack.
6. While the pastries are cooling, make the icing. Combine the powdered sugar and milk until you get the desired consistency. Spread on top of cooled pastries and decorate with sprinkles if desired.

Air Fryer French Toast
Ingredients:
- 4 slices brioche bread
- 2 eggs
- 1/4 cup cream
- 1 tsp vanilla essence
- Cinnamon and sugar
- 80g milk chocolate
- 80ml cream

Directions:
1. Cut bread slices in three fingers, and coat in mixture made from whisked eggs, cream and vanilla. Dip one side of your slice (all around coating and it's too sweet, for me) in cinnamon and sugar before placing in the air fryer, sugared side up. Bake at 200°C for 5 minutes, and turn halfway. No need to wait for the air fryer to heat up - place in as soon as you've put it on. Enjoy with chocolate ganache, heat your cream and throw in your chopped chocolate. Let it sit for a few minutes to melt, then mix through. Enjoy!

Easy Air Fryer Pizza Roll Ups
Servings: 4
Cooking Time: 5 Minutes
Ingredients:
- 4 8 inch flour tortillas
- 4 tablespoons pizza sauce
- 20 slices pepperoni
- 2 mozzarella string cheese
- 1 teaspoon olive oil

Directions:
1. Warm the tortillas: Stack the 4 tortillas onto a microwavable safe plate and place a damp paper towel on top. Microwave for 20 seconds until the tortillas are warm. You can also use a tortilla warmer if you have one.
2. Preheat the air fryer to 375 degrees Fahrenheit and set the time for 5 minutes.
3. Cut the string cheese in half lengthwise.
4. Lay a tortilla flat and add about 1 tablespoon of pizza sauce at the bottom. Add 5 pepperoni slices on top of the pizza sauce, then add the string cheese on top of the pepperoni and roll all of the ingredients into a roll up. Repeat for each tortilla until you have 4 roll ups.
5. Brush the top of each roll up evenly with olive oil as this will add a little extra crispiness to the roll ups.
6. Add the pizza roll ups to the air fryer, seam down, add cook for 5 minutes or until the pizza roll ups are golden brown.
7. Carefully remove the pizza rolls ups from the air fryer, let cool, then enjoy! These taste great dipped in some pizza sauce.

Notes
*Warm up your tortillas before rolling them. This will make them easier to roll without cracking.
*Go easy on the pizza sauce. When assembling the pizza rolls, be sure to use no more than a tablespoon of pizza sauce on each roll up. If you use too much sauce it will just spill out of the tortilla.
*Be sure to let the pizza roll ups cool down before eating as they will be very hot when they first come out of the air fryer.
*Every air fryer is different so be sure to check for doneness halfway through. The air fryer I used to test this recipe was my Instant Vortex Plus 6 quart.
*Store leftovers in the refrigerator in an airtight container for up to 4 days.
*To reheat, preheat the air fryer to 360 degrees Fahrenheit and heat pizza roll ups for 1-2 minutes.

Air Fryer Bread

Servings: 8
Cooking Time: 10 Minutes

Ingredients:
- 2 1/4 teaspoons active dry yeast 1 packet
- 1/4 cup warm water
- 2 cups all purpose flour
- 2 tablespoons granulated sugar
- 1/2 teaspoon salt
- 1/2 cup milk
- 2 tablespoons unsalted butter softened
- Egg Wash
- 1 large egg whisked

Directions:
1. Add yeast to a bowl with water that is warm. Let the yeast sit in the warm water for about 3 to 5 minutes.
2. Once the yeast has activated, add in the flour, sugar, milk, butter, and salt. Gently fold the ingredients together until they were well combined and it becomes slightly flaky.
3. Turn the dough onto a floured surface and knead the dough until it is smooth, then shape it into a ball.
4. Place the ball of dough into the air fryer basket, and then wrap with plastic wrap or a clean kitchen towel. Allow the dough to rest until it doubles in size, about 30 minutes.
5. Brush the top of the loaf with an egg wash. and air fry at 320 degrees Fahrenheit for 8 to 10 minutes, until the top of the bread is golden brown.
6. NOTES
7. Air frying cooking times may vary. Add 1-2 minutes cooking time if necessary, until the top of the bread is golden brown.

Fried Egg In The Air Fryer

Servings: 2
Cooking Time: 5 Minutes

Ingredients:
- 2 large eggs
- Salt and black pepper, to taste

Directions:
1. Spray the insides of 2 small (3- to 4-inch) cake or pie pans with non-stick cooking spray, then place them in the basket of an air fryer.
2. Preheat the air fryer at 350 degrees F for 2 minutes. Crack an egg into each pan and carefully close the air fryer.
3. Cook for 3 minutes until most of the white is set. Lower the heat to 300 degrees F and cook for 1 to 2 minutes until the whites are set but the yolks are still runny.
4. Season with salt and pepper and serve.

Air Fryer Cinnamon Roll Bites

Servings: 4
Cooking Time: 6 Minutes

Ingredients:
- 1 can cinnamon rolls I use Pillsbury

Directions:
1. Open the canned cinnamon rolls, remove the icing to a small bowl, and set it aside.
2. Use a knife to cut the cinnamon rolls into equal pieces. Take each piece of cinnamon

roll and hand roll it until they are small round dough balls.
3. Place the cinnamon roll bites in a single layer into the prepared basket of the air fryer.
4. Air fry cinnamon rolls at 320 degrees Fahrenheit for 6 minutes or until golden brown, flipping the bites halfway through.
5. Carefully remove the cinnamon roll bites from the air fryer basket and serve with the icing as a dipping sauce.

NOTES
I make this recipe in my Cosori 5.8 qt. air fryer or 6.8 quart air fryer. Depending on your air fryer, size and wattages, cooking time may need to be adjusted 1-2 minutes.
Store remaining bites in an airtight container in the refrigerator for up to 3 days. To reheat, add the cinnamon bites back to the air fryer and reheat at 320 degrees Fahrenheit for 1-2 minutes, or until they are heated through.

Air Fryer Pizza Egg Rolls

Servings: 4
Cooking Time: 10 Minutes

Ingredients:
- 8 egg roll wrappers
- 8 mozzarella cheese sticks
- pepperoni slices
- ¼ cup pizza sauce

Directions:
1. Lay out wrappers with corners left and right. Add a small spoonful of pizza sauce onto the center of the eggroll wrapper.
2. Add 3-4 slices of pepperonis, overlapping pieces, then top with a mozzarella cheese stick. Fold bottom corn over the filling and tuck under.
3. Next, fold in the left and right corners, and then turn over, to make a large pillow shape.
4. Lightly spray the air fryer basket, and place each Egg Roll in the basket without stacking or overlapping. Lightly spray each egg roll to help with crispness and color.
5. Air fry at 400 degrees F for 10-12 minutes, until golden and crispy. Turn halfway during the air frying process.
6. Serve with marinara or pizza sauce for dipping. Garnish with parsley flakes.

NOTES
Variations
Add different ingredients - Don't forget that you can easily add your favorite pizza toppings to the middle of these golden brown egg rolls. You can make cheese pizza egg rolls only, or add extra pizza sauce, turkey pepperoni, diced green pepper, black olives, or any other different flavors that you want to add.

Air Fryer Eggs

Servings: 6
Cooking Time: 14 Minutes

Ingredients:
- 6 large eggs or as many as desired
- ice

Directions:
1. Preheat air fryer to 250°F.
2. Place eggs in the air fryer basket (no water needed) in a single layer.
3. For hard-cooked eggs, cook 16-18 minutes.
4. Once the air fryer stops, place the eggs in an ice bath for 5 minutes. Peel under cold running water and enjoy.

Notes
These eggs were tested in a Cosori XL 5.8QT Air Fryer.
Different brands/sizes of air fryers can cook differently so be sure to test one or two eggs before cooking a whole batch of eggs to ensure they're done to your liking. It may take a batch or two to learn your appliance.
Cook times were tested with large eggs directly from the fridge.
For soft eggs cook for 11-12 minutes
For medium jammy eggs cook for 13-14 minutes.
For hard-cooked eggs cook for 16-18 minutes

Air Fryer Pasta Tacos

Servings: 4
Cooking Time: 45 Minutes

Ingredients:
- 24 jumbo pasta shells
- 60ml (1/4 cup) extra virgin olive oil
- 1 small red onion, chopped
- 500g beef mince
- 2 tsp ground cumin
- 2 tsp ground coriander
- 1 tsp garlic powder
- 375g jar medium thick 'n' chunky salsa
- 125g can black beans
- 1 1/2 tsp Mexican chilli powder
- 80g (1 cup) grated cheddar
- 2 tomatoes, diced
- 1 avocado, diced
- Fresh coriander sprigs, to serve
- Sour cream, to serve
- Lime cheeks, to serve
- Select all ingredients

Directions:
1. Cook pasta in a large saucepan of boiling, salted water for 10 minutes or until just tender. Using a slotted spoon, transfer pasta to a tray lined with paper towel to drain.
2. Meanwhile, heat half the oil in a large frying pan over medium-high heat. Add onion. Cook, stirring for 5 minutes or until softened. Add mince. Cook, breaking up mince with a wooden spoon, for 5 minutes or until browned. Add cumin, coriander and half the garlic powder. Cook, stirring for 1 minute or until fragrant. Add salsa and beans. Season with salt and pepper. Bring to a simmer. Reduce heat to low. Simmer for 15 minutes.
3. Preheat air fryer on 200C. Combine Mexican chilli powder, remaining garlic powder and oil in a large bowl. Add pasta. Season well with salt and pepper. Toss gently to coat. Spoon mince mixture in pasta shells to fill. Sprinkle with cheese. Place 1/3 of the pasta shells, cheese-side up, in the air fryer basket. Cook for 5-8 minutes or until shells are golden and crispy. Carefully transfer to a large serving plate. Repeat with remaining pasta.
4. Top with combined tomato and avocado. Sprinkle with coriander. Serve with sour cream and lime cheeks.

Air Fryer Churros

Servings: 6
Cooking Time: 8 Minutes

Ingredients:
- 3/4 cup water
- 1/4 cup butter cut into cubes (4 tbs)
- 1 tablespoon sugar
- 1/2 teaspoon salt
- 1/2 teaspoon ground cinnamon
- 1 cup all purpose flour plus 1-2 tablespoons
- 2 large eggs
- Cinnamon Sugar
- 1/2 cup sugar
- 1 tablespoon ground cinnamon

Directions:
1. In a medium saucepan, add water, butter, sugar, and salt. Heat on medium to high heat until it begins to boil. Stir continuously until butter has melted and sugar and salt are dissolved. Let boil for at least 2-3 minutes.
2. Remove from heat and let mixture cool for about 30 seconds, then add in flour and cinnamon. Then beat in whisked eggs. If dough is too sticky, add in 1-2 extra tablespoons of flour. Dough will be slightly sticky but thick enough to hold shape.
3. Transfer dough to a piping bag with a large star tip. (I use 1M tip)
4. Pipe dough onto baking sheet lined with air fryer parchment paper, into 4-6 inch strips, then place baking sheet in the refrigerator to chill for 30-45 minutes, or freezer for 15 minutes, until dough is firm.
5. Gently transfer parchment paper with piped dough into the air fryer basket. Air fry at 350 degrees for 8-10 minutes, until golden brown.
6. Combine sugar and cinnamon in a small bowl. Brush churros with melted butter,

then toss churros with sugar mixture until well coated.

NOTES

Optional Ingredients: You can dust the churros with powdered sugar, or brown sugar with fall spices. They can also be stuffed with Nutella, peanut butter and jelly, or vanilla pudding.

Kitchen Tips: If you do not have piping bags no worries a resealable plastic bag works just as well. Use a pair of kitchen shears or kitchen scissors to cut one small corner of bag to desired thickness before piping out dough. You can use an electric hand mixer instead of stirring on stovetop if you prefer.

Air Fried Peanut Butter Cups

Servings: 8
Cooking Time: 5 Minutes

Ingredients:
- 8 Reese's Peanut Butter Cups
- 1 can Refrigerated Crescent Rolls 8 rolls

Directions:
1. To make this recipe, begin by unrolling crescent dough and separating each crescent roll.
2. Place one peanut butter cup at the end of the crescent roll and roll until it is completely wrapped. Be sure to pinch dough to cover and seal any exposed parts of the chocolate.
3. Spray Air Fryer basket with nonstick cooking spray, or line with Air Fryer parchment paper. Place wrapped peanut butter cups in the prepared basket, leaving a small space between each pastry.
4. Air fry at 350 degrees for about 5-7 minutes, until crescent rolls are golden brown.
5. Carefully remove them from the Air Fryer. Dust tops with powdered sugar, drizzle with chocolate syrup or frosting glaze.

NOTES

I make these in my Cosori 5.8 Air Fryer. Depending on the size and wattage of the Air Fryer, you may need to add 1-2 additional minutes to cook time.

Leave enough room between each pastry, allowing room for the roll to puff as it cooks.

Do not stack or overlap in the basket. The dough may not cook evenly.

You can make 4 or 8 in a batch, depending on what will fit in your basket.

Air Fried Breakfast Muffins

Ingredients:
- 1 Onion
- 2 Tbsp. of Olive Oil
- 4 Slices of Bacon
- 1 Tsp. of Parsley
- 2 Tsp. of Baking Powder
- 2 Cups of Flour
- 3.5 Oz. of Shredded Cheddar Cheese
- 1 Egg
- 1 Cup of Whole Milk
- Pinch of Salt & Pepper

Directions:
1. Chop 1 onion
2. Saute bacon (optional: chop bacon first)
3. Add the chopped onion when the bacon is almost cooked
4. In a bowl, add parsley, baking powder, flour, and cheddar cheese. Mix well.
5. After mixing, add the egg, olive oil, and milk to the same bowl. Mix well.
6. Add bacon and onions into the mixture.
7. Add a pinch of salt & pepper.
8. Place mixture into each muffin tin and into the air fryer.
9. Cook for 15 minutes at 350 degrees Fahrenheit
10. Enjoy!

Air Fryer Copycat Starbucks Banana Bread

Servings: 8
Cooking Time: 30 Minutes

Ingredients:
- 2 cups all-purpose flour
- 1 teaspoon baking soda
- 1/2 teaspoon salt
- 1 large egg
- 1 1/4 cup granulated sugar
- 1/2 cup vegetable oil
- 2 tablespoons milk

- 1 teaspoon pure vanillla extract
- 3 large ripe bananas
- 1/2 cup diced walnuts optional

Directions:
1. Start by making the mix. In a large mixing bowl, mix the flour, baking soda, salt, egg, and sugar.
2. Then mix in the oil, milk, and vanilla. Mix well.
3. Add the bananas.
4. Mix until smooth. If using walnuts, stir the walnuts in now.
5. Pour the prepared batter into a prepared air fryer-safe pan that has been coated with non-stick cooking spray.
6. Set the temperature to 310 F and the time for 30 minutes. After 30 minutes, check and check for doneness. If it is not done, add another 5 minutes. Until it's fully cooked and a toothpick comes out clean.
7. Once fully cooked, remove the loaf pan from the air fryer basket, and let it cool slightly.
8. Once cooled, slice and serve.
9. Plate, serve, and enjoy!

Air Fryer French Onion Corn On The Cob

Servings: 4
Cooking Time: 25 Minutes

Ingredients:
- 4 corn on the cob
- mayonnaise, to taste
- French onion soup mix, to taste
- dry ranch dressing mix, to taste
- garlic powder, to taste
- black pepper , to taste
- paprika, to taste

Directions:
1. Mix all ingredients, except the corn, together in a bowl. Coat each cob with the mixture and individually
2. wrap each one in aluminum foil. Air fry it at 350°F for 20-25 minutes.
3. You can also bake it in the oven at 375°F for 25 minutes or grill it until the corn is tender.

Air Fryer Blueberry Baked Oats

Servings: 4
Cooking Time: 10-30 Minutes

Ingredients:
- 2 free-range eggs
- 400ml/14fl oz milk
- 4 tbsp runny honey or maple syrup
- 200g/7oz porridge oats
- 2 tsp baking powder
- large pinch salt
- 100g/3½oz fresh blueberries or any frozen berries
- plain yoghurt, to serve (optional)

Directions:
1. Beat together the eggs, milk and honey in a large bowl. Add the oats, baking powder and salt to the bowl, stirring until well mixed. If you have time, leave to sit for 5–10 minutes so the oats can soak up the milk. Preheat the air fryer to 175C.
2. Divide the mixture between four small heatproof dishes or 150ml/5fl oz ramekins and then scatter over the blueberries.
3. Air fry for 10–12 minutes until golden and set. Serve warm or chilled, topped with a spoonful of yoghurt, if using.
4. Recipe Tips
5. Make the mixture the night before and store covered in the fridge to make breakfast even faster in the morning. Remove from the fridge to allow to come to room temperature before topping with blueberries and cooking.
6. If you don't have an air fryer you can bake these in an oven preheated to 200C/180C Fan/Gas 6 for 20-25 minutes.

Air Fryer Egg Rolls
Servings: 4 - 6
Ingredients:
- 1 tbsp. sesame oil
- 1/2 lb. ground pork
- 4 c. coleslaw mix
- 1/2 c. matchstick-cut carrots
- 1 tsp. freshly grated ginger
- 2 garlic cloves, minced
- 3 green onions, sliced
- 2 tsp. soy sauce
- 2 tsp. rice vinegar
- 1/2 tsp. ground black pepper
- 1/4 tsp. kosher salt
- 1/8 tsp. Chinese 5-spice seasoning
- 12 egg roll wrappers
- Nonstick cooking spray
- 1 tbsp. olive oil
- Sweet chili sauce, duck sauce, or hot mustard sauce, for dipping

Directions:
1. Heat the sesame oil in a large skillet over medium heat. Add the pork and cook until crumbled and cooked through, about 4 minutes. Add the coleslaw mix, carrots, ginger and garlic. Cook 2-3 minutes or until the cabbage has wilted. Remove from the heat; stir in the green onions, soy sauce, vinegar, pepper, salt, and 5-spice seasoning. Transfer to a plate and let cool slightly.
2. Place 1 egg roll wrapper on a dry work surface with the points of the wrapper facing up and down (like a diamond). Place about 1/3 cup of the pork mixture in the middle of the wrapper. Dip your fingers in water and and dampen the edges of the wrapper. Fold the left then right points of the wrapper in toward the center. Fold the bottom point over the center. Roll toward the remaining point to form a tight cylinder. Press edges to seal. Place on a plate and cover with a dry towel. Repeat the process with remaining wrappers and pork mixture.
3. Preheat the air fryer to 360°, if required. Spray the air fryer basket with cooking spray. Brush the tops of the egg rolls with olive oil. Working in 3 batches (4 at a time), place the egg rolls in the basket and cook 7 minutes. Flip the egg rolls over and brush with more oil. Cook for an additional 2 minutes.
4. Serve with the dipping sauce of your choice.

Notes
If you have ginger paste in your refrigerator, use 2 teaspoons in place of the 1 teaspoon of freshly grated ginger.

Air Fryer Brisket Tacos
Servings: 4
Cooking Time: 12 Minutes
Ingredients:
- 8 small corn tortillas
- 2 cups leftover beef brisket
- ¼ cup red onions diced
- 1 avocado diced
- 1 lime juiced
- 2 tablespoons cilantro chopped
- toppings as desired for serving

Directions:
1. Preheat the air fryer to 400°F.
2. Wrap the tortillas in foil and place in the air fryer for 3-4 minutes or until warmed. Remove from the air fryer and set aside.
3. While the tortillas are warming, combine avocado, red onion, lime, and cilantro in a bowl. Season with salt an set aside.
4. Chop or pull the brisket into pieces and place in the air fryer. Cook 3-5 minutes or until heated through and it begins to crisp.
5. Top each tortilla with ¼ cup of brisket and a spoonful of the salsa mixture.
6. Drizzle with sour cream and a sprinkle of cheese if desired.

Air Fryer Avocado Eggs
Servings: 2
Cooking Time: 8 Minutes
Ingredients:
- 2 avocados
- 4 eggs
- salt and pepper to taste
- toppings optional: Salsa, Shredded Cheese, Crumbled Bacon, Hot Sauce

Directions:

1. Line the air fryer basket with parchment paper and set aside.
2. Slice avocado in half, lengthwise, and then carefully remove the pit.
3. Using a spoon, gently remove some of the avocado meat, forming a well where the pit was. Save the removed avocado to top the egg, or to eat separately.
4. Place halves in the air fryer basket, and then carefully crack eggs, breaking direction into each half of the avocado.
5. Air fry at 400 degrees F for 8-12 minutes, depending on how well done you prefer your eggs.
6. Season as desired.

NOTES
Variations

Make an avocado toast - If you want to spread the cooked cream avocado on toast and add a bit of Bagel seasoning, you can create an avocado mixture on bread in no time at all. Simple ingredients can easily make all sorts of an easy breakfast.

Add feta cheese - Putting feta cheese on top of the fried egg sounds awesome. This is a simple way that you can make air fryer-baked eggs with an avocado half taste different easily.

Make it spicy - Add some sweet chili sauce to the top of avocado eggs for a spicy hot flavor combination. You can skip the sweet and add red pepper flakes as well.

Pair with other breakfast foods - Make it a large meal by adding some hash browns, turkey bacon, or even fresh fruit.

Air Fryer Zucchini Pizza Bites

Servings: 4
Cooking Time: 10 Minutes

Ingredients:
- 2 zucchini (medium sized)
- ¾ cup Primal Kitchen's Roasted Garlic Marinara Sauce
- ¾ cup shredded mozzarella cheese
- ½ cup turkey pepperoni
- 1 tbsp olive oil (for spraying)

Directions:
1. Slice the zucchini into slices that are about ¼ inch thick.
2. Lay the zucchini slices flat in the air fryer basket. Do not overcrowd. The zucchini should not overlap. You will need to do this in batches. Spray the slices with olive oil and cook for 3-4 minutes at 400 degrees F.
3. Add the marinara sauce, shredded mozzarella cheese and turkey pepperoni on top of each zucchini slice.
4. Place the basket back into the air fryer and cook for 4-6 minutes at 400 degrees F or until the cheese melts.
5. Repeat as many times as needed depending on the size of your air fryer. As you are making them, let them cool on a wire cooling rack.

Air Fryer Mini Egg, Ham, And Cheese Quiche

Servings: 6
Cooking Time: 25 Minutes

Ingredients:
- 4 eggs
- 2 tbsp milk
- ½ cup diced ham or bacon, sausage
- ½ cup cheese shredded
- ½ teaspoon salt & pepper

Directions:
1. Preheat the air fryer to 350°F.
2. Combine all of the ingredients in a bowl and whisk until combined.
3. Place the silicone cups in the air fryer basket and evenly divide the egg mixture filling up the cups 3/4 of the way full.
4. Cover with foil and bake for 20 minutes. Then uncover and cook for 5 more.

BEEF, PORK & LAMB RECIPES

Air Fryer Bacon Wrapped Corn On The Cob
Servings: 2-4
Cooking Time: 20 Minutes

Ingredients:
- 2-4 ears fresh corn, shucked and cleaned
- 2-8 slices bacon, depending on how much corn & if you do double bacon or not
- salt, to taste
- black pepper, to taste
- oil spray or olive oil

Directions:
1. If needed, cut ends of corn to fit into your air fryer basket/tray. Or for smaller air fryers, cut the corn in half.
2. Coat all sides of the corn with light oil spray (if you're using only 1 bacon strip/ear). If needed, make sure to spray the ends of the corn is where it can often get dry.
3. Wrap bacon around the corn. Skewer one toothpick to secure each end of bacon to corn. Skewer the toothpick side-ways into the corn and bacon so it does't stick up too much. Season with salt and pepper to taste.
4. For 2 corn - Air Fry at 380°F for 10 minutes. Flip the corn. Continue Air Frying for another 3-8 minutes or until bacon is crisp and corn is tender.
5. For 4 corn - Air Fry at 380°F for 10 minutes. Flip the corn. Continue Air Frying for another 6-10 minutes or until bacon is crisp and corn is tender. (Cooking time will depend on size of corn, thickness of the bacon, how full air fryer basket is, & different models/sizes of air fryers).
6. If needed, flip once more and Air Fry for a couple more minutes or until the bacon is crispy on all sides.
7. Remove toothpicks before eating. Add butter if desired and enjoy!

Air Fryer Pork Chops In 9 Minutes
Servings: 4
Cooking Time: 9 Minutes

Ingredients:
- 4 medium pork chops boneless
- 1 tablespoon olive oil
- 2 teaspoons smoked paprika
- 2 teapoons cumin
- 1 teaspoon onion powder
- 1/2 teaspoon salt
- 1/2 teaspoon pepper

Directions:
1. Preheat the air fryer to 190C/375F.
2. Pat dry the boneless pork chops, then add into a bowl and rub the oil generously over them all.
3. Mix the spices in a bowl, then rub on both sides of the pork.
4. Place the pork chops in the air fryer basket and cook for 9 minutes, flipping halfway through.
5. Remove the pork from the air fryer and serve immediately.

Notes
TO STORE: Use air-tight containers to refrigerate the pork chops. They will keep well for up to five days.
TO FREEZE: Place leftovers in a ziplock bag and store them in the freezer for up to two months.
TO REHEAT: Either microwave the chops for 20-30 seconds or reheat in a non-stick pan until hot.

Air Fryer Bbq Chops

Ingredients:
- 500g chops washed and cleaned, pat dry
- 1 teaspoon crushed garlic
- 1/2 teaspoon crushed green chilli
- 1/2 teaspoon salt
- 1/2 teaspoon onion powder
- 1/2 teaspoon garlic powder
- 1/4 cup spare rib marinade
- 1/4 cup BBQ sauce

Directions:

1. Marinate chops in above ingredients, allow to marinate overnight. In drawer 1 add in your chops, set the air fryer on air-fry, 180 degrees celsius for 20 minutes. On turn food prompt baste chops with left over marinate.
2. In drawer 2, place your pre-cooked garlic bread, air-fry for 2 minutes on 180 degrees celsius, to melt butter and bread to soften. And then press the synch finish button. This feature allows both drawers to finish cooking at the same time.
3. Serve immediately with all your favourite braai sides, enjoy.

Air Fryer Bacon Wrapped Dates
Servings: 3
Cooking Time: 10 Minutes

Ingredients:
- 6 pieces of bacon
- 4 ounces cream cheese
- 1 tsp cinnamon
- 18 Medjool pitted dates

Directions:
1. Slice bacon pieces into halves. Set aside.
2. Slice open the tops of the dates and remove the pits if not already pitted.
3. In a small bowl, mix together the cream cheese and cinnamon.
4. Carefully spoon ½ teaspoon of the cinnamon and cream cheese mixture into each date.
5. Wrap each date with a piece of the bacon, and carefully secure the bacon with a toothpick if needed.
6. Air fry the bacon-wrapped dates at 350 degrees Fahrenheit for 10 minutes or until the bacon is cooked fully.
7. Carefully remove the stuffed dates from the air fryer and serve.

NOTES
These are so simple to serve! You can add them to a charcuterie board for a fun treat or serve them up on a platter at your next party.
I do think that this delicious appetizer is best eaten fresh, but you can always store it for later. Let the stuffed date cool down all the way, and then add any leftovers to an airtight container. Place the container in the fridge and keep it cool. Eat within 2 days for the best flavor.

Air Fryer Roast Pork Belly
Servings: 1
Cooking Time: 1 Hour

Ingredients:
- 2 teaspoons fennel seeds
- 2 teaspoons sea salt flakes
- 2 teaspoons dried chilli flakes
- 2 teaspoons finely grated lemon rind
- 2 teaspoons cloves garlic, crushed
- 1 teaspoon olive oil
- 1 kilograms piece boneless pork belly, rind scored
- to serve: extra sea salt flakes, roast potatoes and roast shallots

Directions:
1. Preheat a 7-litre air fryer to 180°C/350°F for 3 minutes.
2. Place fennel seeds, salt and chilli flakes in a mortar and pestle; crush lightly. Add lemon rind, garlic and oil; pound to combine. Pat pork belly rind dry with paper towel. Rub fennel mixture all over pork.
3. Taking care, place pork, skin-side up, in the air fryer basket. Reset the temperature to 200°C/400°F; cook for 25 minutes until skin crackles.
4. Reset the temperature to 160°C/325°F; cook pork for a further 25 minutes until tender or an internal temperature of 70°C–75°C/158°F–167°F is reached on a meat thermometer. (If pork is overbrowning, cover with foil.)
5. Thickly slice pork and sprinkle with extra salt flakes; serve with any cooking juices from the bottom of the air fryer pan, roast potatoes and roast shallots.

3-ingredient Air Fryer Bacon-cream Cheese Crescents

Servings: 8

Ingredients:
- 1 can (8 oz) refrigerated Pillsbury™ Original Crescent Rolls (8 Count)
- 1/3 cup chive & onion cream cheese spread (from 8-oz container)
- 8 slices cooked bacon, cut in half

Directions:
1. Cut 8-inch round of cooking parchment paper. Place in bottom of air fryer basket.
2. Unroll dough; separate into 8 triangles. Spoon and spread 2 teaspoons cream cheese spread onto each triangle. Top with 2 stacked bacon halves. Roll up, starting at shortest side and rolling to opposite point. Place 3 to 4 crescents on parchment paper in air fryer basket point side down, spacing apart.
3. Set air fryer to 325°F; cook 6 to 7 minutes or until crescent tops are light brown. With tongs, turn over each one; cook 2 to 3 minutes or until golden brown and cooked through. Remove from air fryer. Repeat with remaining crescents.

Air Fryer Taco Casserole

Servings: 4
Cooking Time: 20 Minutes

Ingredients:
- 1 lb lean ground beef 95% lean
- 3 tbsp taco seasoning
- 1/4 cup water
- 1/2 cup bell pepper chopped
- 10 oz diced tomatoes and green chilis not drained
- 4 large eggs
- 1/4 cup sour cream
- 1/3 cup heavy cream
- 1/2 cup cheddar cheese shredded
- 1 tbsp green onions optional

Directions:
1. Brown the lean ground beef in a skillet over medium heat, about 5 minutes or until no longer pink. Drain.
2. Add the water, taco seasoning, diced bell pepper, and canned tomatoes with green chilis. Stir and simmer for 3 minutes.
3. Preheat the Air Fryer to 300 degrees Fahrenheit. Prepare the air fryer casserole/cake dish.
4. In a medium mixing bowl, whisk the eggs, sour cream, and heavy cream together. Set aside.
5. Pour the taco meat mixture into the bottom of the prepared casserole pan. Top the meat mixture with the egg mixture.
6. Place the casserole into the air fryer basket and cook for 18 minutes. Top with cheese and cook an additional 2 minutes, or until the cheese is fully melted.
7. Top with green onions and serve.

NOTES
Store in an airtight container in the refrigerator for up to 3 days.
Consider adding additional flavors like diced jalapenos for extra spice.
Mix up the flavors by adding a little mozzarella and cream cheese to the dish.

Air Fryer Prosciutto Wrapped Asparagus

Servings: 4
Cooking Time: 8 Minutes

Ingredients:
- 1 pound asparagus
- 6 ounces prosciutto

Directions:
1. Preheat air fryer to 400°F.
2. Wash and trim the end of the asparagus.
3. Wrap one slice of prosciutto around one asparagus and place in the air fryer basket.
4. Cook for 7-8 minutes or until asparagus is tender and prosciutto is crispy.

Air Fryer Bacon Wrapped Brussel Sprouts

Servings: 4
Cooking Time: 13 Minutes

Ingredients:
- 8 slices bacon regular and sliced in half
- 16 small Brussels sprouts
- ¼ cup brown sugar

Directions:
1. Wrap one slice of halved bacon around each brussels sprout, seal with a toothpick if necessary. Repeat until all sprouts have been wrapped.
2. In a large glass bowl, toss wrapped sprouts with brown sugar, until they are well coated.
3. Place in the air fryer basket, without stacking or overlapping.
4. Air Fry at 380 degrees F for 13-16 minutes, until bacon is crispy.

NOTES
Variations
Change up the flavor of bacon - You can use salty bacon, crispy bacon, thick cut bacon, or any piece of bacon or strip of bacon that you want. Maple bacon sounds like some pretty good strips of bacon to add to this easy recipe!

Add toppings - Let's be truthful here and say that toppings are always a crowd-pleaser. Drizzling some olive oil with salt and black pepper on top of this delicious appetizer adds taste in an easy way.

You can add soy sauce to these tender brussels sprouts after they are done cooking, or add some sweetness with a drizzle of maple syrup!

Air Fryer Armadillo Eggs

Servings: 6
Cooking Time: 15 Minutes

Ingredients:
- 1 pound pork sausage ground
- 1 pound bacon 12 slices
- 6 medium jalapenos
- 4 ounces cream cheese room temperature
- 1/2 cup shredded cheddar cheese
- 1 cup Honey BBQ Sauce

Directions:
1. Rinse the jalapeno peppers and pat dry, then slice in half. Remove stems, membrane, and seeds, then set aside.
2. In a medium bowl, combine the cheddar and cream cheese. Generously spoon the cream cheese mixture into one of the halves of the jalapeno and then place two halves together.
3. Divide the pork sausage into six even portions. Flatten a portion of the sausage and fold around a jalapeno, pinch meat to completely seal and cover jalapeno, while shaping into an oval egg shape. Repeat until all jalapenos are covered with sausage.
4. Wrap each covered jalapeno with two slices of bacon, wrapping each piece of bacon with tight wrap, securing with toothpicks.
5. Place in the air fryer basket and air fry at 380 for 15-17 minutes until sausage reaches an internal temperature of 160 degrees F and bacon is crispy. Use a meat thermometer to confirm doneness.
6. Using a basting brush or spoon, brush egg with barbecue sauce before serving.

NOTES
VARIATIONS and TIPS:
You can use flavored bacon like smoky bacon or Hickory bacon.
For higher heat level, and spicy peppers, leave some of the membrane.
There are other types of cheese blend you can add for a creamy cheese mixture. Shredded Monterey jack, mozzarella cheese, pepper jack, or even Mexican blend cheese, will make this a perfect appetizer recipe.
Dip in hot sauce, or for more flavor, try a Korean BBQ sauce or Raspberry Chipotle Sauce.
For a larger crowd, double batch recipe!

Air Fryer Taco Ring

Servings: 6
Cooking Time: 6 Minutes

Ingredients:
- 1/2 pound lean ground beef
- 1/4 cup water
- 2 tablespoons taco seasoning mix
- 1 cup shredded cheddar cheese
- 1 can crescent rolls

Directions:
1. In a medium skillet, cook ground beef on medium to high heat until meat is completely browned.
2. Remove from heat and drain excess grease out of the skillet. Add water and taco seasoning, stirring to coat meat. Add any additional taco ring mix-ins, such as jalapeños or onions.
3. Line the air fryer basket with a piece of parchment paper.
4. Open the can of crescent rolls, separate each roll and then lay out rolls on the parchment paper, so they are slightly overlapping at larger ends of the triangles to form a round sun shape.
5. Evenly spoon the ground beef around the center of the crescent roll circle. Then top beef with cheese, along with optional fillings such as onions or jalapenos.
6. Next lift the tops of each crescent roll over the beef mixture, and tuck under the circle, so it is sealed, and mixture will not come out.
7. Air fry at 350 degrees F for 6-8 minutes until dough has completed the cooking process and is golden brown.
8. Carefully lift the taco ring out of the basket and serve individual taco crescents while hot.

NOTES
Optional Favorite Toppings: Diced green onions, ripe olives, refried beans, queso cheese, chopped tomato, crispy tortilla chips, sweet corn, shredded lettuce, black beans or salsa.
Optional Favorite Dipping Sauce: Hot sauce, bit of nacho cheese, garlic aioli, sour cream, guacamole or salsa Verde.

Substitutions: Monterey jack, ground chicken, a cheese stick, Mexican cheese, ground turkey or cream cheese.

Air Fryer Korean-inspired Pork Tenderloin Lettuce Wraps

Servings: 2-4

Ingredients:
- 1 lb. pork tenderloin
- 3/4 tsp. kosher salt
- 1/4 c. gochujang (Korean hot pepper paste)
- 1 clove garlic, finely grated
- 2 tbsp. honey
- 1 tbsp. toasted sesame oil
- 1/4 tsp. finely grated fresh ginger
- 1 tbsp. unseasoned rice vinegar
- Olive oil cooking spray
- 1 head of Bibb or butter lettuce, leaves separated
- Sliced cucumber, sliced scallions, and cooked rice, for serving

Directions:
1. Cut pork in half crosswise; season all over with salt.
2. In a medium bowl, combine gochujang, garlic, honey, oil, and ginger. Transfer 1/4 cup gochujang mixture to a small bowl and stir in vinegar; set aside for serving. Add pork to bowl with remaining sauce and toss to coat.
3. Lightly coat an air-fryer basket with cooking spray. Place pork in basket and cook at 350°, turning occasionally, until pork is golden brown and an instant-read thermometer inserted into thickest part registers 140°, 16 to 19 minutes. Let rest about 10 minutes before slicing.
4. Place pork in lettuce leaves, along with cucumber, scallions, and rice. Serve with reserved sauce alongside.

Air Fryer Bacon Wrapped Brussels Sprouts

Servings: 8
Cooking Time: 7 Minutes

Ingredients:
- 1 pound brussels sprouts
- ½ pound bacon
- ⅓ cup maple syrup

Directions:
1. Preheat the air fryer to 375°F.
2. Wash and trim brussels cutting them in half.
3. Cut each piece of bacon into thirds. Wrap bacon around the brussels sprouts.
4. Place seam side down in the air fryer basket and brush with maple syrup.
5. Bake 7-10 minutes or until bacon is crisp and brussels sprouts are tender.

Notes
Brussels sprouts should be cooked in a single layer. If needed, cook in batches.

Air Fryer Steak Bites

Servings: 4
Cooking Time: 6 Minutes

Ingredients:
- 1 pound sirloin steak or strip loin or ribeye
- 1 tablespoon vegetable oil
- 1 tablespoon soy sauce
- 1 ½ teaspoons Worcestershire sauce
- 2 cloves garlic minced
- 1 tablespoon melted salted butter
- salt & pepper to taste
- 1 tablespoon fresh parsley

Directions:
1. Cut steak into 1-inch cubes. Toss with oil, soy sauce, Worcestershire sauce, garlic, salt & pepper. Marinate 15 minutes.
2. Preheat air fryer to 400°F.
3. Remove the steak bites from the marinade and dab dry. Toss with melted butter.
4. Add steak bites to the air fryer basket in a single layer and cook 6-7 minutes or until browned. Do not overcook.
5. Toss with parsley and additional butter if desired. Serve with horseradish sauce below.

Notes
Cook steak bites in batches if needed. Do not overcrowd the air fryer.
Whisk together the following for Horseradish Dipping Sauce:
¼ cup sour cream
2 tablespoons mayonnaise
1 ½ tablespoons prepared horseradish
1 teaspoon fresh lemon juice
1 small clove garlic
salt & pepper to taste

Air Fryer Herb Crusted Roast Beef

Servings: 6
Cooking Time: 1 Hour 20 Minutes

Ingredients:
- 1.2 kg piece beef scotch fillet
- 1 tablespoon olive oil
- 2/3 cup (80g) panko breadcrumbs
- ¼ cup (20g) finely grated parmesan
- 2 tablespoon chopped flat-leaf parsley
- 1 tablespoon chopped tarragon
- ¼ cup chopped chives
- 2 cloves garlic, crushed
- ¼ cup (70g) wholegrain mustard
- 1 teaspoon smoked paprika
- olive oil cooking spray
- 150 grams swiss brown mushrooms, halved (or quartered if large)
- 150 grams button mushrooms, halved (or quartered if large)
- ¾ cup (180ml) thickened cream
- to serve: roast potatoes

Directions:
1. Preheat a 7-litre air fryer to 200°C/400°F for 5 minutes.
2. Brush beef with 2 teaspoons of the the oil and season.
3. Taking care, place beef in the air fryer basket; at 200°C/400°F, cook for 15 minutes, turning halfway through cooking time, until browned all over.
4. Meanwhile, combine the breadcrumbs, parmesan, parsley, tarragon, half the chives and half the garlic in a bowl, then season. Transfer beef to a plate and pat dry with paper towel. Working quickly, spread 2

tablespoons of the mustard over the top and sides of the beef, sprinkle with paprika, then firmly press on breadcrumb mixture. Spray breadcrumbs generously with cooking spray.
5. Return beef to the air fryer basket, then cover basket tightly with foil. Reset the temperature to 180°C/350°F; cook for 30 minutes. Remove foil.
6. Toss mushrooms in remaining oil and add to the air fryer basket with beef; cook, without foil, for a further 10 minutes until beef is medium or cooked to your liking (see testing meat when ready to right) and mushrooms are browned. Transfer beef to a dish; cover loosely with foil and rest for 15 minutes.
7. Meanwhile, to make creamy mushrooms, combine cream and remaining garlic and mustard in a medium saucepan over medium heat; add the mushrooms and any
8. cooking juices from the bottom of the air fryer pan and bring to the boil. Reduce heat; simmer, stirring occasionally, for 5 minutes or until sauce thickens slightly.
9. Stir in remaining chives and season to taste.
10. Thinly slice beef and serve with creamy mushrooms and roast potatoes.testing meat when readyInsert a meat thermometer into the thickest part of the beef. The internal temperature should reach:
11. rare 55–60°C/130–140°F
12. medium–rare 60–65°C/140–150°F
13. medium 65–70°C/150–160°F
14. medium–well done 70–75°C/160–170°F
15. well done 75°C/170°F

Air Fryer Boneless Pork Chops

Servings: 2 - 2

Ingredients:
- 2 8 oz boneless pork chops (1.25" thick)
- Kosher salt and freshly ground black pepper
- 2 tsp. pork rub (optional)

Directions:
1. Set air fryer to 400F and preheat 3 to 4 minutes. Pat pork chops dry, and season both sides with salt and pepper and/or a spice rub.
2. Place pork chops into heated air fryer and cook, 6 minutes.
3. Flip chops and cook until internal temperature on an instant read thermometer reads 135F-145F, 5-8 minutes. If it's not warm enough, continue cooking, checking every 2-3 minutes, until cooked through.
4. Cover chops with a tent of aluminum foil and let rest 5 minutes, to allow chops to reabsorb juices, before slicing and eating.

Air Fryer Ham Steaks

Servings: 1
Cooking Time: 10 Minutes

Ingredients:
- 1 ham steak
- 2 tablespoons butter, melted
- 2 tablespoons brown sugar, packed
- 1 teaspoon honey* (optional)

Directions:
1. Preheat your air fryer to 380 degrees.
2. Remove the ham steak from its packaging.
3. Mix the brown sugar and melted butter together in a bowl.
4. Place ham steak in the air fryer and baste half of the mixture on top of the ham slice.
5. Cook for 10-12 minutes, flipping and basting the ham steak again halfway through.
6. Remove from the air fryer and drizzle optional honey on top.

NOTES
*add honey only if not using a honey ham

Air Fryer Candied Bacon

Servings: 4
Cooking Time: 10 Minutes

Ingredients:
- 1 pound bacon
- ¼ cup brown sugar

Directions:
1. Place bacon slices in a shallow dish with brown sugar. Toss bacon slices well so both sides are coated with brown sugar.
2. Place slices in the air fryer basket, working in batches so they don't overlap while air frying.
3. Air fry at 380 degrees F for 10-12 minutes until bacon is crispy. Remove slices and place on a cooling rack or on a plate to cool before eating.

NOTES

No matter if you call this millionaire bacon or billionaire bacon, everyone will agree that this pig candy is yummy! I like to use dark brown sugar for this recipe as it makes it a delicious treat.

Cooking the bacon in the air fryer is also a great way to keep the bacon grease separate from the bacon, as it will fall through the bottom of the air fryer basket.

But did you know that you can actually use that leftover bacon grease for other air fryer recipes and cooking recipes? I'll save it and store it in a jar and then use it for cooking at other times. (It's really good to use when you're popping popcorn!)

Air Fryer Bacon

Servings: 2
Cooking Time: 10 Minutes

Ingredients:
- 3 strips of bacon any thickness

Directions:
1. First, preheat the air fryer to 350°F.
2. Next, slice each strip of bacon in half and lay them on your air fryer pan next to each other. They can be overlapping a little bit, but not all the way.
3. Air fry bacon at 350°F for: thin bacon: 6-7 minutes, medium bacon: 8 minutes, or thick bacon: 9-10 minutes. Flip bacon halfway through the bake time. If you like your bacon crispy, continue cooking for an extra 30 seconds to 1.5 minutes depending on the thickness of your bacon.

Tips & Notes

If you are planning to cook multiple rounds of bacon, make sure to discard excess grease that will build up on the bottom of your air fryer pan. This is to prevent smoking.

Make sure to keep an eye on your bacon as it can burn easily. The 350°F temperature should help prevent smoking, so don't cook your bacon any higher than that.

Air Fryer Chuck Roast

Servings: 6
Cooking Time: 45 Minutes

Ingredients:
- 2 pounds beef chuck roast
- 1 tablespoon olive oil
- ½ tablespoon Worcestershire sauce
- 1 ½ teaspoons kosher salt
- 1 ½ teaspoons garlic powder
- 1 teaspoon onion powder
- 1 teaspoon dried thyme
- 1 teaspoon dried rosemary
- 1 teaspoon black pepper

Directions:
1. Line the inside of your air fryer with aluminum foil. Preheat the air fryer to 390 degrees F.
2. In a small bowl, whisk together olive oil and Worcestershire sauce. In a second small bowl, combine the salt, garlic powder, onion powder, thyme, rosemary, and pepper.
3. Rub the roast with the olive oil-Worcestershire sauce mixture, then rub the herb mixture over the entire roast. Place the roast in the basket of your air fryer.
4. Air fry for 15 minutes, then carefully flip the roast. Air fry at 320 degrees F for another 45-60 minutes, depending on the size of the roast.

5. Remove, allow to rest for 10 minutes, then slice and serve with your favorite sides.

Air Fryer Corn Ribs
Servings: 4
Cooking Time: 12 Minutes

Ingredients:
- 2 ears of corn fresh
- 1 Tablespoon butter unsalted
- 1/4 teaspoon garlic powder
- 1/4 teaspoon salt Kosher
- 1/2 teaspoon smoked paprika
- 1/2 teaspoon ground black pepper
- 1/2 teaspoon dried parsley
- fresh parsley for garnish

Directions:
1. Take each whole ear of corn, remove from the husk.
2. Rub cobs to remove the corn silks from in between the corn kernels and cut off the ends.
3. Place corn on the cobs in a microwave safe bowl covered with a damp paper towel and microwave for 2 minutes.
4. Let corn cobs cool for 5 minutes on a chopping board or until they are cool enough to touch.
5. Use a sharp knife and slice into the corn cobs: cut the corn in halves lengthwise, and then cut halves into quarters, to make 4 pieces per cob of corn.
6. In a small bowl, combine butter, garlic powder, salt, paprika, black pepper and dried parsley.
7. Brush the corn ribs with the seasoning mixture, coating entire corn rib well.
8. In a single layer place the seasoned corn ribs into the air fryer basket.
9. Air fry at 400 degrees F for 12 minutes, flipping halfway through the cooking process.
10. Top with fresh parsley before serving.

NOTES
Optional Favorite Dipping Sauce: Ranch dressing, sour cream and chives, Carolina style bbq sauce, chipotle mayo or Greek yogurt with red pepper flakes.
Optional Additional Toppings: Lime wedges, fresh cilantro, fresh coriander or minced garlic butter.
Cooking Tips: Use a pastry brush to apply butter mixture to pieces of corn ribs. Cutting the corn into ribs makes it easier to eat especially for the little ones. For crispier corn cook for an additional 1-2 minutes.
Optional Additional Seasonings: Chili powder, lime juice, taco seasoning, chili oil, Elote seasoning, onion powder, cayenne pepper, chipotle powder or smoked salt.

Ribs
Servings: 4
Cooking Time: 25 Minutes

Ingredients:
- 3 lb baby back ribs, or pork loin ribs
- 6 cups apple juice
- 1/4 cup apple cider vinegar
- 1/2 tsp liquid smoke, optional
- 1 tbsp. seasoning salt, (Johnny's or Lawry's)
- 2 Tbsp BBQ dry rub
- 2/3 cup sweet BBQ sauce, divided

Directions:
1. Pat dry the rack of ribs with a paper towel and rub on your dry ingredients on both sides.
2. In the Instant Pot, combine apple juice, vinegar, liquid smoke and 1/3 cup of bbq sauce.
3. Coil the rack of ribs inside the with the bone-side facing the center. Ribs should all be partially submerged. Cook on high pressure for 25 min followed by a 10 min natural pressure release before manually releasing remaining pressure.
4. Using two sets of tongs, carefully transfer ribs to a rimmed baking sheet lined with a wire rack with the meat side up. Brush the top and sides with the remaining 1/3 cup bbq sauce. Broil in the center of the oven on high for 4-5 min*. Remove from the oven and let rest for 5-10 min before serving. Serve with more bbq sauce if desired.

Notes

*To Finish Ribs on the Grill: Preheat the grill to 350-400°F. Place ribs directly on preheated grill, cover, and grill 5 min.

*To Finish Ribs in the Air Fryer: Cut rack in half and place both halves side by side in the air fryer basket for 4 min on high.

Air Fryer Steak
Servings: 4
Cooking Time: 12 Minutes

Ingredients:
- 4 8-oz Top sirloin steaks (at least 1 inch thick, preferably 1.5 inches; other high-quality steaks with similar thickness will also work)
- 2 tsp Sea salt
- 1/2 tsp Black pepper
- 1/2 recipe Compound butter (optional)

Directions:
1. Remove your steak from the fridge about 30 minutes before cooking to bring it to room temperature. (This will ensure even cooking.)
2. Make compound butter according to the instructions here. Refrigerate until ready to serve.
3. Preheat the air fryer to 400 degrees F (204 degrees C).
4. Pat the steaks dry with paper towels. Season the steaks liberally with sea salt and black pepper on both sides.
5. Arrange the steaks in the air fryer in a single layer, so the pieces are not touching or only minimally touching (cook in batches if needed; don't crowd the basket). Air fry until the steaks reach your desired doneness (use a probe thermometer for best results). For 1.5-inch thick steaks, that's about 10-12 minutes for rare, 11-13 minutes for medium rare, 12-14 minutes for medium, 13-15 minutes for medium well, or 14-16 minutes for well done. Use a meat thermometer to check for the right temperature – 120 degrees F (52 degrees C) for rare, 130 degrees F (54 degrees C) for medium rare, 140 degrees F (60 degrees C) for medium, 150 degrees F (66 degrees C) for medium well, or 160 degrees F (71 degrees C) for well done. The temperature will rise by another 5 degrees F while resting (see next step).
6. Remove the steaks from the air and transfer to a plate. Top each with 1 tablespoon (14g) of compound butter.
7. Let the steaks rest for 5 minutes before slicing against the grain.

Air Fryer Short Ribs
Servings: 2-4
Cooking Time: 15 Minutes

Ingredients:
- 1 pound short ribs (pork or beef), 1.5-inch pieces
- 1 tablespoon vegetable oil
- 1 tablespoon soy sauce (or oyster sauce)
- 1 tablespoon Shaoxing wine (optional)
- 1/2 teaspoon salt
- 1/2 teaspoon ground black pepper
- 1/2 teaspoon garlic powder
- 1/2 teaspoon paprika
- 1/4 teaspoon ground cumin powder
- 1/4 teaspoon crushed red pepper (optional)
- 1 teaspoon cornstarch

Directions:
1. In a large mixing bowl or Ziploc bag, combine the ribs with all the ingredients and mix well to coat evenly. If you use the Ziploc bag, press the seasoning around to coat evenly. Let the marinated ribs rest for at least 15 minutes to soak in all the flavour.
2. Place the marinated ribs in a single layer in the air fryer basket. Cook at 350F for 13-15 minutes until golden brown and crispy. Shake the basket halfway to cook the ribs evenly. (See recipe tips for oven bake and deep fry instructions).
3. Serve immediately with your favorite dipping sauce, such as spicy mayo, sweet chili sauce, ketchup, or ranch.

NOTES
How to bake in the oven: Place the marinated short ribs in a single layer on a parchment-lined quarter sheet baking pan and bake at 400F for 15-20 minutes until crispy and golden brown.

How to deep fry: Heat oil in a medium cooking pot (at least 2-inches deep) over medium high heat for 3-4 minutes until the oil shimmers. Deep fry the marinated ribs until golden brown, about 5-7 minutes. Turn the ribs occasionally to get an even golden crust on all sides. Transfer the ribs on a paper towel lined plate to drain excess oil.

How to store: Keep air fryer short ribs in an airtight container in the fridge for up to 3-4 days.

How to reheat: Reheat these dry short ribs in the air fryer at 350F for 5 to 10 minutes until warm and crispy. You can also reheat them in a 350F preheated oven for 10 to 15 minutes.

Air Fryer Ham With Pineapple Glaze

Servings: 10
Cooking Time: 1 Hour 20 Minutes

Ingredients:
- 2-3 pounds (907 - 1360 g) boneless, fully cooked ham
- PINEAPPLE JUICE GLAZE
- 1 cup (240 ml) pineapple juice
- 1/2 cup (110 g) brown sugar , or to taste
- 1/2 teaspoon (2.5 ml) ground cinnamon
- 1/4 teaspoon (1.25 ml) ground cloves (optional)
- 1/2 teaspoon (2.5 ml) salt , or to taste
- 3 pineapple rings
- Optional - (a few maraschino cherries or cranberries for garnish)
- Aluminum Foil
- 8" square Baking Pan

Directions:
1. Remove the ham from the fridge and allow to come up to room temperature, about 2 hours before cooking.
2. Make the Glaze: Add pineapple juice, brown sugar, cinnamon, optional ground cloves and salt to pan. Simmer on medium-low heat for about 20 minutes or until is reduced to about half or until it starts to thicken a bit. Remove from heat.
3. If needed, remove the netting from the ham. If ham is not pre-sliced, score the ham with shallow 3/4-inch criss-cross cuts.
4. For Basket Style Air Fryers: Line the air fryer basket with 2 pieces of long, criss-crossed foil sheets. Lay the ham on top of the foil and then brush with some of the glaze to coat the ham. Close the foil over the ham and wrap tightly.
5. For Oven Style Air Fryers: Place the ham in an 8"x8" baking pan which fits in your air fryer (you may need to trim the edges of the ham to fit your pan and air fryer size). Brush with some of the glaze and close foil over the ham, wrapping tightly.
6. Air Fry at 340°F/170°C for 25 minutes. Open the foil and brush the ham with more glaze (make sure to reserve some glaze for finishing & serving).
7. Close the foil tightly, and Air Fry again at 340°/170°C for 25 minutes. After air frying for the 50 minutes, open up the foil again and now push the foil down around the edges of the ham if using the basket-style air fryer method. Create a boat with the foil that holds the juices and keeps the hand from drying out. If using the Oven Style Air Fryer method, just remove the foil from the 8"x8" pan.
8. Add the slices of pineapple on the top of the ham. Spread more glaze over everything.
9. Increase heat to Air Fry at 360°F/180°C for about 5 minutes, or until caramelized to your liking. Let ham rest for 5 minutes before serving. Place the the maraschino cherries or cranberries in the center of the pineapple rings for optional garnish.
10. Optional serving: Combine the juices from the air fryer basket and the remaining glaze in a saucepan. Bring to a simmer and cook for a couple minutes or until slightly thickened. Brush the glaze onto the ham when serving or serve in a bowl.

Air Fryer Brown Sugar Pork Chops
Servings: 4
Cooking Time: 12 Minutes
Ingredients:
- 4 boneless center cut pork chops 1 ½ – 2 inches thick
- 2 tablespoons brown sugar
- 1 tablespoon paprika
- 1 ½ teaspoons salt
- 1 ½ teaspoons fresh ground black pepper
- 1 teaspoon ground mustard
- ½ teaspoon onion powder
- ¼ teaspoon garlic powder
- 2 tablespoons olive oil

Directions:
1. Preheat air fryer to 400°F on bake.
2. Pat pork chops dry with a paper towel.
3. In a small bowl, mix together all the dry ingredients.
4. Coat the pork chops with olive oil and rub in the mixture.
5. Cook pork chops for 12 minutes, flipping pork chops over after 6 minutes.

Notes
Leftover pork chops will keep in an airtight container in the refrigerator for up to 4 days.

Air Fryer Crispy Chilli Beef
Servings: 2
Cooking Time: 15 Minutes
Ingredients:
- 250g thin-cut minute steak, thinly sliced into strips
- 2 tbsp cornflour
- 2 tbsp vegetable oil, plus a drizzle
- 2 garlic cloves, crushed
- thumb-sized piece of ginger, peeled and cut into matchsticks
- 1 red chilli, thinly sliced
- 1 red pepper, cut into chunks
- 4 spring onions, sliced, green and white parts separated
- 4 tbsp rice wine vinegar or white wine vinegar
- 1 tbsp soy sauce
- 2 tbsp sweet chilli sauce
- 2 tbsp tomato ketchup
- For the marinade
- ? tsp Chinese five-spice powder
- 2 tsp soy sauce
- 1 tsp sesame oil
- 1 tsp caster sugar

Directions:
1. First, combine the marinade ingredients in a bowl. Add the steak strips and toss to coat. Leave in the fridge for up to 24 hrs if you can, or carry on to step 2.
2. Sprinkle the cornflour over the steak and mix until each piece is coated in a floury paste. Pull the strips apart and arrange over a plate. Drizzle each piece of steak with a little oil. Heat the air fryer to 220C if it has a preheat setting.
3. Carefully put the beef on the cooking rack in the air fryer, cook for 6 mins, then turn and cook for another 4-6 mins until crispy.
4. Meanwhile, heat 2 tbsp vegetable oil in a wok over a high heat and stir-fry the garlic, ginger, chilli, pepper and white ends of the spring onions for 2-3 mins until the pepper softens. Be careful not to burn the ginger and garlic. Add the vinegar, soy, sweet chilli sauce and tomato ketchup, mix well and cook for another minute until bubbling.
5. Tip the beef into the wok and toss through the sauce. Continue cooking for another minute until piping hot, then serve scattered with the spring onion greens and a little extra sauce on the side.

Air Fryer Beef Empanadas
Servings: 8
Cooking Time: 16 Minutes
Ingredients:
- 8 Goya empanada discs (in frozen section, thawed)
- 1 cup picadillo
- 1 egg white (whisked)
- 1 teaspoon water

Directions:
1. Spray the air fryer basket generously with olive oil spray to avoid sticking, or line the basket with air fryer parchment paper.

2. Place 2 tablespoons of the picadillo in the center of each disc. Fold in half and use a fork to seal the edges. Repeat with the remaining dough.
3. Whisk the egg whites with water, then brush the tops of the empanadas.
4. Air fry in a single layer, in batches as needed 350F 8 minutes, turning halfway or until golden. Remove from heat and repeat with the remaining empanadas.

Notes

How to Bake Empanadas in the Oven: If you don't have an air fryer, you can also bake them in the oven at 400 degrees on a nonstick baking sheet for about 18 to 20 minutes until golden.

How to Freeze Empanadas: You can flash freeze the uncooked empanadas on a sheet pan. Once frozen, transfer to a freezer-safe container for up to 3 months.

Air Fry From Frozen: Pop the frozen empanadas right into your air fryer and air fry 350F for about 12 minutes, turning halfway until golden and hot.

Air Fryer Bacon Wrapped Serranos

Ingredients:
- 12 Serrano peppers
- 12 Slices partially Cooked bacon
- 2 String Mozarella Cheeses

Directions:
1. Partially cook the bacon in the air fryer at 300° for 3 minutes on each side. Place onto paper towel and set aside.
2. Cut the tops off the serrano peppers and carefully slice down one side of the pepper(do not cut all the way through). Fold open the pepper and remove seeds.
3. Peel pieces of the string cheese and stuff the peppers. Wrap the bacon around each pepper tightly then place into air fryer basket.
4. Air fry at 350° for 5 minutes or until desired bacon crispiness.

Air Fryer Grilled Ham And Cheese

Servings: 4
Cooking Time: 7 Minutes

Ingredients:
- 2 tablespoons mayonnaise
- 8 slices white bread
- 2 tablespoons Dijon mustard
- 8 slices deli ham
- 4 large slices Swiss cheese
- 8 dill pickle slices
- cooking spray

Directions:
1. Spread mayonnaise on one side of each slice of bread. With mayo side down, lightly spread 4 slices of bread with Dijon mustard, evenly top each with Swiss cheese, ham slices, folded to fit, and pickle slices. Place the remaining 4 bread slices on the sandwiches, mayo side up, and lightly press sandwiches to close.
2. Preheat the air fryer to 380 degrees F (193 degrees C). Spray the air fryer basket with cooking spray or line with a parchment liner.
3. Place sandwiches in the air fryer basket in a single layer, leaving some space around them. You may have to cook the sandwiches in batches, depending on the size of your fryer.
4. Cook until sandwiches begin to brown, 3 to 4 minutes. Flip, and cook until cheese has melted and sandwiches are golden brown, 2 to 3 minutes more. Slice sandwiches in half and serve warm.

Note:

Mayonnaise is the only thing I use these days on grilled sandwiches. It's always ready, spreads easily, browns beautifully, and has no mayo flavor. But you can use butter, if you prefer. Air fryer cooking times may vary depending on the brand and size. So watch your sandwiches closely, especially toward the end of cooking.

SANDWICHES & BURGERS RECIPES

Keto Friendly Game Day Burgers

Ingredients:
- Mini Beef Burgers:
- 1.5 pounds ground beef
- 1/4 cup onion, diced
- 1 tsp salt
- 1/4 tsp pepper
- 1 tsp brown Mustard
- Low Carb Sauce:
- 1/2 cup mayonnaise
- 1 tsp white wine vinegar
- 1 tsp paprika
- 1 tsp garlic powder
- 1 tsp onion powder
- 4 tbsp dill pickle relish

Directions:
1. Using your hands mix together the beef, onion, salt, pepper, and brown sugar (optional.)
2. Form into 15-20 mini balls.
3. Cook in your air fryer, flipping half way to your desired doneness, 7-8 minutes at 390 degrees.
4. While the burgers are cooking, mix your mayonnaise, white vinegar, paprika, garlic powder, onion powder, and dill pickle relish together. Set to the side.
5. Place each burger on a skewer with cheese, lettuce, pickles, and the special sauce.
6. Enjoy!

Air Fryer Hamburgers

Servings: 4
Cooking Time: 8 Minutes

Ingredients:
- 1-pound ground beef, thawed (preferably 80/20)
- 1 clove garlic, minced
- 1/2 teaspoon salt
- 1/4 teaspoon pepper

Directions:
1. Preheat air fryer to 360 degrees.
2. Mix together the ground beef, minced garlic, salt, and pepper with your hands.
3. Form ground beef into 4 patties and press them down with the back of a pie plate to make them evenly flat.
4. Place hamburgers in a single layer inside the air fryer.
5. Cook for 8-12 minutes, flipping halfway through cooking for medium-well hamburgers.*
6. Carefully remove hamburgers from the air fryer,** place onto hamburger buns (if using), and add desired toppings.

NOTES
*thicker hamburgers may take longer to cook if not pressed down properly
** if making cheeseburgers, place a piece of cheese on each burger in the air fryer, turn the air fryer off, and let the burgers sit in the air fryer for 1 to 2 minutes until melted

Air Fried Crispy Chicken Sandwiches

Servings: 4

Ingredients:
- 2 large chicken breasts, cut in half and pounded to an even thickness
- 1 cup buttermilk
- 1 tablespoon kosher salt or 1 teaspoon table salt
- ¾ cup panko breadcrumbs
- ½ cup all-purpose flour
- ½ teaspoon salt
- ¼ teaspoon dried oregano
- ½ teaspoon paprika
- ¼ teaspoon garlic powder
- ¼ teaspoon dried thyme
- ¼ teaspoon ground ginger
- ½ teaspoon ground black pepper
- Oil spray
- 4 brioche burger buns
- Assorted toppings such as lettuce, tomato, onions and additional condiments

Directions:
1. Place the chicken breasts in a zipper top bag and pour in buttermilk and salt. Squeeze the air out and seal the bag. Marinate in the

refrigerator for at least an hour or preferably overnight.
2. In a shallow bowl combine the panko breadcrumbs, flour and spices.
3. Remove the chicken breasts from the buttermilk. Remove excess buttermilk and dredge in the breadcrumb mixture.
4. Arrange the chicken breasts in one layer on a parchment-lined baking sheet, thoroughly coating chicken with oil spray on both sides.
5. Air Fry at 375°F for 20 – 25 minutes or until internal temperature reads 165°F and the chicken breasts are golden brown and crispy. For more even cooking, flip the chicken halfway through and spray with more oil if desired.
6. Serve chicken sandwiches on toasted brioche buns with lettuce, tomatoes, red onion and other favorite condiments.

Air Fryer Grilled Cheese Sandwich
Servings: 2
Cooking Time: 7 Minutes
Ingredients:
- 8 slices white bread
- 1 tablespoon butter
- 4 slices cheese

Directions:
1. Spread a light layer of the butter on one side of each piece of bread.
2. Place the buttered side down in the air fryer basket.
3. Cover the slice of bread with a piece of cheese. Then top the cheese with another slice of bread, with the buttered side up.
4. Air Fry at 370 degrees F for 3-5 minutes. Then flip, and air fry for 2-3 additional minutes, until bread reaches desired crispness.

NOTES
Make this a heartier meal by adding a few slices of bacon to the sandwich, avocado slices, or on inside of slices, spread bread with pesto sauce before adding cheese.
Depending on the type of bread you use, you may want to adjust the cook times. For softer bread, or French Bread, air fry until it reaches your desired crispness.

Air Fryer Bacon, Egg And Cheese Biscuit Breakfast Sandwiches
Servings: 8
Ingredients:
- 1 can (16.3 oz) refrigerated Pillsbury™ Grands!™ Southern Homestyle Original Biscuits (8 Count)
- 6 eggs
- 1/4 teaspoon salt
- 1/8 teaspoon pepper, if desired
- 1 tablespoon butter
- 8 slices cooked bacon, cut in half crosswise
- 8 slices (3/4 oz each) American cheese

Directions:
1. Spray bottom of air fryer basket with cooking spray. Separate dough into 8 biscuits. Place 4 biscuits in air fryer basket, spacing apart.
2. Set air fryer to 330°F; cook 6 minutes. Using tongs or spatula, turn over each biscuit. Cook 4 to 5 minutes or until biscuits are deep golden brown and cooked through. Remove from air fryer; cover loosely with foil to keep warm while cooking second batch. Cook remaining biscuits as directed above.
3. Meanwhile, in medium bowl, beat eggs, salt and pepper thoroughly with fork or whisk until well mixed. In 10-inch skillet, heat butter over medium heat just until butter begins to sizzle. Pour egg mixture into skillet. Cook until set, stirring occasionally.
4. To serve, split warm biscuits; top bottom half of each with scrambled eggs, bacon and cheese. Cover with top halves of biscuits.

Air Fryer Frozen Burger

Servings: 2
Cooking Time: 15 Minutes

Ingredients:
- 2 frozen burger patties

Directions:
1. Place frozen burgers in a single layer in the basket of the air fryer.
2. Air fry the burgers at 350 degrees Fahrenheit for 15 minutes, flipping the burgers halfway through cook time.
3. If desired, add sliced cheese during the last minute of cooking time.
4. Carefully remove the burgers from the air fryer and serve them with your favorite toppings.

NOTES
If adding cheese, top with sliced cheese during the last minute of cook time.
Serve bunless for a healthier burger.

Air Fryer Chicken Burgers

Servings: 4
Cooking Time: 10 Minutes

Ingredients:
- 1 pound ground chicken
- 1 large egg
- 1 cup mozzarella cheese shredded
- 1/2 cup onion finely chopped
- 1/2 cup panko breadcrumbs
- 1 teaspoon minced garlic
- 1/2 teaspoon kosher salt
- 1/4 teaspoon ground black pepper

Directions:
1. Preheat air fryer to 365 degrees F.
2. In a large bowl, combine the chicken, egg, cheese, onion, panko crumbs, garlic, salt and pepper. Mix chicken mixture together with your hands until fully combined.
3. Divide the chicken mixture into 4 equal parts and shape them into 5-inch diameter burgers.
4. Spray the air fryer basket with non-stick cooking spray and place the chicken patties in air fryer in a single layer.
5. Air fry the chicken burgers at 365 degrees F for 8-10 minutes or until cooked through, depending on the thickness of the patties.
6. Use a meat thermometer to confirm internal temperature of burger patties which should be a safe temperature of 165 degrees F.
7. Allow chicken burgers to cool for a couple of minutes then carefully remove them from the basket.
8. Serve while hot or let them continue to rest on a baking rack.

NOTES
Optional Additional Favorite Sauces: BBQ sauce, mustard yogurt sauce, chili sauce, ketchup, spicy sriracha sauce (based on your spice level), honey mustard, marinara sauce, relish or a sweet and spicy pickle.
Optional Favorite Toppings: Shredded lettuce, slice of tomato, raw or caramelized onions, sundried tomato strips, bacon, avocado, pepper jack cheese, American cheese or shredded cheese.
Cooking Tips: Use a silicone mat to make it an easy clean up and prevent food sticking to your basket. For crispy chicken patties brush a little olive oil on the patties prior to placing them in your air fryer.
I make this recipe in my Cosori 5.8 qt. air fryer. Depending on your air fryer, size and wattages, your cooking time may need to be adjusted 1-2 minutes.

Greek Lamb Burgers With Baked Eggplant Fries

Servings: 4

Ingredients:
- Nonstick cooking spray
- 1 pound ground lamb
- 2 ounces feta cheese, crumbled (about ½ cup)
- ½ cup grated red onion (from 1 small onion), divided
- 1 ½ tablespoon olive oil, divided
- 2 ½ teaspoons kosher salt, divided
- ¾ teaspoon freshly ground black pepper, divided
- 1 ½ cups panko

- 2 large egg whites
- 1 medium eggplant, cut into ½-by-1-by-2-in. wedges
- ½ cup grated English cucumber (from ½ cucumber)
- 1 cup plain whole-milk Greek yogurt
- 2 teaspoons fresh lemon juice (from 1 lemon)
- Hamburger buns and lettuce, for serving

Directions:
1. Preheat oven to 425°F. Lightly coat a rimmed baking sheet with cooking spray. Stir together lamb, cheese, ¼ cup onion, 1 tablespoon oil, 1 teaspoon salt, and ½ teaspoon pepper in a bowl until just combined; shape into 4 patties.
2. Combine panko and remaining 1½ teaspoons salt in a large ziplock plastic bag. Whisk egg whites in a large bowl until foamy. Dip eggplant wedges, 1 at a time, in egg whites and transfer to bag with panko. Once all eggplant has been added to bag, seal and shake well to coat. Arrange eggplant in an even layer on prepared baking sheet and coat generously with cooking spray. Bake until golden brown, about 20 minutes, flipping halfway through.
3. Meanwhile, heat remaining ½ tablespoon oil in a large nonstick skillet over medium-high. Add lamb patties and cook, flipping once, until browned, about 4 minutes per side for medium.
4. Place cucumber and remaining ¼ cup onion on a paper towel. Squeeze gently to release liquid. Transfer to a small bowl and stir in yogurt, lemon juice, and remaining ¼ teaspoon pepper.
5. Place patties on buns with lettuce and yogurt sauce. Serve with eggplant fries and remaining yogurt sauce.

Air Fryer Biscuit Egg Sandwiches
Servings: 4

Ingredients:
- Deselect All
- Nonstick cooking spray, for the molds
- 4 large eggs
- Kosher salt
- 4 thin slices deli ham
- One 16.3-ounce tube refrigerated flaky biscuit dough, such as Pillsbury
- Hot sauce, for serving

Directions:
1. Special equipment: 4 silicone baking cups, 6-quart air fryer
2. Spray 4 silicone baking cups with nonstick spray. Transfer the cups to the basket of a 6-quart air fryer.
3. Whisk together the eggs in a large glass measuring cup until no white streaks remain. Season with 1/2 teaspoon salt. Divide the eggs among the baking cups. Insert a piece of ham into each cup, crumpling it to make it fit (some of the ham should stick out above the surface of the eggs).
4. Tear off 4 biscuits from the tube of dough. Place each biscuit in the basket of the air fryer in a single layer. Set the air fryer to 300 degrees F and cook for 10 minutes. The biscuits should be golden brown; transfer to a cutting board.
5. Gently lift each egg muffin from its mold so you can see if it's set. If there's no liquid egg on the bottom, transfer the mold to the cutting board. If there is liquid egg on the bottom, cook for up to 1 minute more.
6. Slice each biscuit in half crosswise. Remove the egg muffins from the molds and slice in half crosswise. Arrange the two egg halves on each bottom biscuit, drizzle with plenty of hot sauce and sandwich with the top biscuit.

FISH & SEAFOOD RECIPES

Air Fryer Honey Mustard Salmon Recipe

Servings: 3
Cooking Time: 10 Minutes

Ingredients:
- 3 salmon fillets 1 ½ inches thick
- salt and pepper
- 2 tablespoons honey
- 1 tablespoon Dijon mustard

Directions:
1. Make a foil sling for the air fryer basket, about 4 inches tall and a few inches longer than the width of the basket. Lay foil widthwise across basket, pressing it into and up the sides. Lightly spray foil and basket with cooking spray.
2. Pat salmon dry with paper towels. Season with salt and pepper.
3. In a small bowl, mix together honey and Dijon, until well combined. Reserve 1 tablespoon of glaze. Drizzle remaining glaze evenly over salmon fillets, tops and sides.
4. Arrange fillets skin side down on sling in the basket, with space between them. (The number of fillets you can fit in your air fryer at one time depends on the size of the fillets and the size of your air fryer.)
5. Cook at 350°F/175°C for 8-10 minutes, until salmon flakes easily and registers at 145°F/62.8°C (thinner salmon will be ready sooner, thicker salmon will take more time).
6. Using sling, carefully lift salmon from air fryer. Loosen the skin with a fish spatula or utensil, then transfer fillets to plate, leaving skin behind.
7. Drizzle reserved sauce over fillets. Garnish with fresh parsley, if desired. Serve warm.

Air Fryer Mahi Mahi

Servings: 3-4
Cooking Time: 12 Minutes

Ingredients:
- 1 to 1 1/2 pounds mahi mahi fillets
- 2 tablespoons olive oil
- 2 cups panko breadcrumbs
- 1 teaspoon paprika
- 1/2 teaspoon garlic powder
- 1/2 teaspoon onion powder
- 1/2 teaspoon salt
- 1/2 teaspoon pepper
- OPTIONAL
- Lemon wedges, for serving

Directions:
1. Preheat your air fryer to 400 degrees.
2. Place the mahi mahi fillets on a large plate and drizzle or baste with olive oil.
3. In a shallow dish, mix the panko breadcrumbs, paprika, garlic powder, onion powder, salt, and pepper.
4. Dip each mahi mahi fillet into the panko mixture then place in a single layer in the air fryer basket. Spritz with cooking oil.
5. Cook for 12 to 15 minutes, flipping the mahi mahi halfway through cooking.
6. Remove them from the air fryer, serve with lemon wedges, and enjoy!

NOTES
HOW TO REHEAT MAHI MAHI IN THE AIR FRYER
Preheat your air fryer to 350 degrees.
Place the leftover mahi mahi in the air fryer and cook for about 3 to 4 minutes until heated thoroughly.
HOW TO COOK FROZEN MAHI MAHI IN THE AIR FRYER
Preheat your air fryer to 400 degrees.
Place the fillets in a single layer and cook for 13 to 14 minutes until heated thoroughly. Flip the mahi mahi halfway through cooking. If the fish is breaded, spritz with oil once at the beginning and once halfway through.

Air Fryer Oven Cheesy Scalloped Potatoes

Ingredients:
- 3 tablespoons butter
- 1 small white or yellow onion, peeled and thinly sliced
- 4 large garlic cloves, minced
- 1/4 cup all-purpose flour
- 1 cup chicken stock or vegetable stock
- 2 cups milk (2% or whole milk, recommended)
- 1 1/2 teaspoons Kosher salt
- 1/2 teaspoon black pepper
- 2 teaspoons fresh thyme leaves, divided
- 10 Yukon Gold Potatoes, sliced into 1/8-inch rounds
- 2 cups freshly-grated sharp cheddar cheese*, divided
- 1/2 cup freshly-grated Parmesan cheese, plus extra for serving

Directions:
1. Prep oven and baking dish: Pre-heat air fryer to 400°F. Grease a 8 x 8-inch baking dish with cooking spray, and set it aside.
2. Sauté the onion and garlic. Melt butter in a large sauté pan over medium-high heat. Add onion, and sauté for 4-5 minutes until soft and translucent. Add garlic and sauté for an additional 1-2 minutes until fragrant. Stir in the flour until it is evenly combined, and cook for 1 more minute.
3. Simmer the sauce. Gradually pour in the stock, and whisk until combined. Add in the milk, salt, pepper, and 1 teaspoon thyme, and whisk until combined. Continue cooking for an additional 1-2 minutes until the sauce just barely begins to simmer around the edges of the pan and thickens. Then remove from heat and set aside.
4. Layer the potatoes. Spread half of the sliced potatoes in an even layer on the bottom of the pan. Top evenly with half of the cream sauce. Then sprinkle evenly with 1 cup of the shredded cheddar cheese, and all of the Parmesan cheese. Top evenly with the remaining sliced potatoes, the other half of the cream sauce, and the remaining 1 cup of cheddar cheese.
5. Bake: Cover the pan with aluminum foil and bake at 400 degrees for 40 minutes. The sauce should be nice and bubbly around the edges. Then remove the foil and bake uncovered for 10-15 minutes, or until the potatoes are cooked through.
6. Cool. Transfer the pan to a cooling rack, and sprinkle with the remaining teaspoon of thyme and extra Parmesan.
7. Serve. Serve warm.

Air Fryer Crispy Fish Fillets

Servings: 3
Cooking Time: 15 Minutes

Ingredients:
- 1 pound (454 g) white fish fillets (cod, halibut, tilapia, etc.)
- 1 teaspoon (5 ml) kosher salt , or to taste
- 1/2 teaspoon (2.5 ml) black pepper , or to taste
- 1 teaspoon (5 ml) garlic powder
- 1 teaspoon (5 ml) paprika
- 1-2 cups (60-120 g) breading of choice breadcrumbs, panko, crushed pork rinds or almond flour
- 1 egg , or more if needed
- Cooking Spray
- EQUIPMENT
- Air Fryer
- Air Fryer Parchment Paper (optional)
- Perforated Silicone Mats (optional)

Directions:
1. Preheat the Air Fryer at 380°F/193°C for 4 minutes.
2. If using frozen filets, make sure to thaw first. Cut fish filets in half if needed. Make sure they are even sized so they'll cook evenly. The thicker they are, the longer they will take to cook. Pat the filets dry. Lightly oil the filets and then season with the salt, black pepper, garlic powder, and paprika.
3. Put the breading in a shallow bowl. In another bowl, beat the eggs. Dip the filets in the egg, shaking off excess egg. Dredge the filets in your breading of choice. Press filets

into the bowl of breading so that they completely coat the filets. Repeat this process for all fish pieces.
4. Line air fryer basket or tray with perforated parchment paper or perforated silicone mat (highly recommended - if you don't have perforated parchment paper or mat, make sure to generously coat the air fryer basket with oil spray). Lightly spray parchment paper with oil spray. Lay coated fish in a single layer on the parchment (cook in batches if needed). Generously spray all sides of the breaded filets with oil spray to coat any dry spots.
5. Air Fry at 380°F/193°C for 8-14 minutes, depending on the size and thickness of your filets. After 6 minutes, flip the filets. Lightly spray any dry spots than then continue cooking for the remaining time or until they are crispy brown and the fish is cooked through. Serve with your favorite dip: tartar sauce, mustard, aioli, etc.

Air Fryer Fried Shrimp
Servings: 4

Ingredients:
- Deselect All
- Fried Shrimp:
- 1 pound large shrimp (16/20 count), peeled and deveined, tails on
- Kosher salt and freshly ground black pepper
- 1/2 cup all-purpose flour
- 2 large eggs
- 1 cup panko breadcrumbs
- Nonstick cooking spray, for the shrimp
- Spicy Remoulade Sauce:
- 1/2 cup mayonnaise
- 2 tablespoons chopped pickled jalapenos
- 2 tablespoons whole grain mustard
- 1 tablespoon ketchup
- 1 tablespoon hot sauce
- 1 scallion, thinly sliced

Directions:
1. For the fried shrimp: Pat the shrimp dry between a couple paper towels, then season with a pinch of salt and a few grinds of pepper.
2. Whisk the flour with 3/4 teaspoon salt and few grinds of pepper in a shallow bowl or baking dish. Whisk the eggs with a pinch of salt in another shallow bowl. Add the panko to a third shallow bowl. Dip a shrimp in the seasoned flour, shaking off any excess, then dip in the beaten eggs. Dredge in the panko, turning until evenly coated. Transfer to a large plate or a rimmed baking sheet and repeat with the remaining shrimp.
3. Preheat a 5 quart air fryer to 385 degrees F. Working in batches, place some of the shrimp in a single layer in the fryer basket, then spray lightly with cooking spray. Cook, flipping halfway through, until the shrimp are golden brown and cooked through, about 10 minutes.
4. For the spicy remoulade sauce: Meanwhile, stir together the mayonnaise, pickled jalapenos, mustard, ketchup, hot sauce and scallion in a small bowl until smooth. Serve with the fried shrimp for dipping.

Cook's Note
You may need to fry the shrimp in 2 to 3 batches, depending on the size of your air-fryer basket.

Frozen Shrimp In The Air Fryer
Servings: 4
Cooking Time: 7 Minutes

Ingredients:
- 1 pound frozen cooked large shrimp
- 1 tablespoon unsalted butter, melted
- 1 tablespoon Old Bay seasoning
- ½ tablespoon lemon juice
- 1 teaspoon minced garlic

Directions:
1. Heat air fryer to 350 degrees F.
2. Break apart frozen shrimp and place the shrimp, butter, Old Bay seasoning, lemon juice, and garlic in a large bowl. Stir to combine and coat all of the shrimp.
3. In a single layer lay your shrimp (about ½ a pound per batch) and cook for 6 to 7 minutes until fully heated.

Air Fryer Coconut Shrimp

Servings: 4

Ingredients:
- FOR THE SHRIMP
- 1/2 c. all-purpose flour
- Kosher salt
- Freshly ground black pepper
- 1 c. panko bread crumbs
- 1/2 c. shredded sweetened coconut
- 2 large eggs, beaten
- 1 lb. large tail-on shrimp, peeled and deveined
- 1/2 c. mayonnaise
- 1 tbsp. sriracha
- 1 tbsp. Thai sweet chili sauce

Directions:
1. In a shallow bowl, season flour with salt and black pepper. In another shallow bowl, combine panko and coconut. In a third shallow bowl, beat eggs to blend.
2. Working one at a time, dip shrimp into seasoned flour, shaking off any excess. Dip into eggs, then into panko mixture, gently pressing to adhere.
3. Working in batches if necessary, in an air-fryer basket, arrange shrimp in a single layer. Cook at 400° until shrimp is golden brown and cooked through, 7 to 9 minutes.
4. In a small bowl, combine mayonnaise, sriracha, and chili sauce.
5. Arrange shrimp on a platter. Serve with dipping sauce alongside.

Air Fryer Lobster Tail

Servings: 4
Cooking Time: 5 Minutes

Ingredients:
- 4 5-oz Lobster tails
- 1/4 cup Salted butter (melted; 1/2 stick)
- 2 cloves Garlic (crushed)
- 2 tsp Lemon juice
- 1/2 tsp Smoked paprika
- 1 pinch Cayenne pepper (or more if you want extra heat)

Directions:
1. If tails are frozen, thaw them overnight in the fridge, or in a bag submerged in cold water on the counter for about 30 minutes.
2. Preheat the air fryer to 400 degrees F (204 degrees C) for a few minutes.
3. Butterfly the lobster tails. Using kitchen shears, cut down the center of the shell lengthwise, starting from the end opposite the tail fins, continuing down until you reach the tail but without cutting the tail. You want to cut through the top of the shell, but don't cut through the bottom shell. Use your thumbs and fingers to spread open the shell on top, then use your thumbs and fingers to spread open the shell. Run a bamboo skewer through the center of the flesh lengthwise to prevent curling.
4. In a small bowl, whisk together the melted butter, garlic, lemon juice, smoked paprika, and cayenne. Brush the butter mixture over the lobster meat.
5. Cook lobster tails in the air fryer for 5-6 minutes for 5-ounce lobster tails, or until the meat is opaque and internal temperature in the thickest part reaches 140 degrees F (60 degrees C). (If your tails are a different size, a good rule of thumb for lobster tail air fryer time is about 1 minute per ounce of individual tail. For example, if your lobster tails are 8 ounces each, you'll air fry them for about 8 minutes.) After cooking for 1 minute per ounce of individual tail, check the internal temperature with a meat thermometer and if they are not done yet, cook for 1-3 more minutes as needed.

Cajun Air Fryer Fish

Ingredients:
- Fresh fish fillets. Use any sustainable white fish. I used hake but halibut, cod, tilapia, bass, grouper, haddock, snapper or catfish will all work well.
- Olive oil - Vegetable oil like avocado oil is a good substitution
- Cajun seasoning/Cajun spice. Most supermarkets will have a cajun spice blend in their spice aisle.

- Smoked paprika
- Garlic powder. Onion powder can also be used
- Fresh lemon juice

Directions:
1. Slice the fish into portions then place in the air fryer basket. In a small bowl, mix the olive oil, lemon juice and seasonings together then spoon over the fish. I don't usually add parchment paper to the basket but you can if you're worried about the fish sticking. You can also spray the basket with cooking spray or olive oil. Air fry for 8-10 minutes at 200°C/400°F until the fish is caramelized on the outside and opaque and juicy on the inside. Cooking time will depend on the thickness of the fish but generally fish is cooked when it flakes apart easily and a fork can be inserted without any resistance. Remove from the air fryer then serve with lemon wedges.

Air Fryer Scallops

Servings: 4
Cooking Time: 5 Minutes

Ingredients:
- 1/2 lb scallops
- 1/2 teaspoon salt
- 1/4 teaspoon pepper
- 2 tablespoons butter divided
- 1/4 cup parsley finely chopped
- 1/2 small lemon sliced

Directions:
1. Pat dry the scallops and then sprinkle with salt and pepper. Brush one tablespoon of butter over the scallops.
2. Generously grease an air fryer basket with cooking spray and add a single layer of scallops.
3. Air fry at 200C/400 for 5-7 minutes, flipping halfway through.
4. Remove them from the air fryer basket, and brush more butter on them. Sprinkle with finely chopped parsley and serve with sliced lemon.

Notes

TO STORE: Place leftover scallops in a shallow container and store them in the refrigerator for up to two days.
TO FREEZE: Once the scallops have cooled to room temperature, place them in a shallow container and store them in the freezer for up to two months.
TO REHEAT: Reheat in the air fryer or microwave until warm.

Fish 'n' Chips

Servings: 4

Ingredients:
- For the chips
- 700g King Edward or Maris Piper potatoes
- 2 tbsp sunflower oil
- Sea salt
- 2 tsp semolina (optional)
- lemon wedges and parsley to garnish
- For the fish
- 2 slices stale bread, crusts removed and torn into pieces
- 1 garlic clove
- 1 zest of lemon
- 5g fresh parsley, leaves and stalks
- sea salt and pepper to taste
- 1 x 120g chunky thick skinless cod fillets, pat dry
- 2 tbsp oil
- COOKING MODE
- When entering cooking mode - We will enable your screen to stay 'always on' to avoid any unnecessary interruptions whilst you cook!

Directions:
1. Peel potatoes and cut into 5cm thick chips. Place in a bowl, cover with water and allow to soak for 30 minutes to remove excess starch. Rinse and pat potatoes dry.
2. In a clean bowl, add chips, oil, salt and semolina. Toss together to make sure the chips are coated. Insert crisper plates into both drawers and add the chips to Zone 1 drawer.
3. Place bread, garlic, lemon, parsley and seasoning into a food processor. Whizz until you have fine breadcrumbs. Add oil

and pulse until mixed. Spoon breadcrumb topping onto cod. Press topping on with the back of spoon. Spray Zone 2 drawer and carefully place topped cod into drawer.
4. Select Zone 1, turn the dial to select AIR FRY, set temperature to 200°C, and set time to 26 minutes. Select Zone 2 and turn the dial to select ROAST, set temperature to 170°C and set time to 14 minutes. Select SYNC. Press the dial to begin cooking.
5. After 10 minutes, shake Zone 1 drawer, shake again after 15 and 20 minutes. Check at 24 minutes if cooked enough.
6. When cooking time is complete, remove fish and chips and serve with tartar sauce and mushy peas.

Air-fryer Salmon With Teriyaki Glaze

Servings: 4
Cooking Time: 10 Minutes

Ingredients:
- 460g skinless salmon fillets
- 1/4 cup teriyaki sauce
- 450g microwave long-grain white rice
- 350g Asian-style salad kit
- 3 tsp sesame seeds, toasted
- 2 spring onions, thinly sliced

Directions:
1. Preheat air fryer to 200°C for 3 minutes. Place salmon in a shallow dish. Pour over sauce and turn to coat. Line air fryer basket with baking paper, trimming to fit. Using tongs, place salmon in paper-lined basket. Slide pan and basket into appliance. Set timer for 8 minutes. Cook, basting with any remaining sauce halfway through cooking time, or until cooked to your liking.
2. Meanwhile, heat rice according to packet instructions. Prepare salad according to kit instructions.
3. Transfer rice to a bowl. Stir in two-thirds of the sesame seeds. Divide rice mixture and salad among bowls. Top with salmon and any cooking juices. Serve scattered with onion and remaining sesame seeds.

Crisp-skinned Air Fryer Salmon With Salsa Verde

Servings: 4
Cooking Time: 25 Minutes

Ingredients:
- 4 x 185g salmon fillets, skin on
- 1 tablespoon extra virgin olive oil
- 2 teaspoon sea salt flakes
- 1 small shallot, chopped finely
- 1 clove garlic, crushed
- 2 teaspoon finely grated lemon rind
- 2 tablespoon lemon juice
- 2 tablespoon finely chopped dill
- ¼ cup chopped flat-leaf parsley
- 2 tablespoon chopped chives
- 1 tablespoon baby capers, chopped coarsely
- to serve: extra sea salt flakes

Directions:
1. Preheat a 7-litre air fryer to 200°C/400°F for 3 minutes.
2. Rub salmon with oil, then sprinkle with salt flakes.
3. Taking care, line the air fryer basket with a silicone mat, if available. Place salmon, skin-side up, in the basket; at 200°C/400°F, cook for 8 minutes until skin is crisp and salmon is cooked to your liking.
4. Meanwhile, to make salsa verde, combine remaining ingredients in a medium bowl; mix well. Season.
5. Serve salmon topped with salsa verde and sprinkled with extra salt flakes.

Air Fryer Shrimp

Servings: 4
Cooking Time: 7 Minutes

Ingredients:
- 1 lb shrimp large or extra large
- 1 tablespoon olive oil
- 1/2 tablespoon lemon juice
- 1/2 teaspoon salt
- 1/2 teaspoon pepper
- 1/2 teaspoon garlic
- 1/2 teaspoon smoked paprika
- 1 teaspoon Italian seasonings

Directions:
1. Pat dry shrimp with a paper towel.
2. In a mixing bowl, whisk together the olive oil and lemon juice. Add the seasonings and mix well. Toss through the shrimp in the seasoning mix.
3. Cook the shrimp at 200C/400F for 7-8 minutes.
4. Serve immediately.

Notes

TO STORE: Air fryer shrimp can be stored in the refrigerator for up to 3 days in an air-tight container.
TO FREEZE: Place leftovers in a ziplock bag and store it in the freezer for up to 2 months.
TO REHEAT: Thaw and then put on the baking sheet or in the air fryer basket to reheat until crispy.

Air Fryer Shrimp Skewers
Servings: 4
Cooking Time: 9 Minutes

Ingredients:
- 20 large shrimp fresh, peeled

Directions:
1. Soak the wooden skewers in water for 20 minutes.
2. Rinse the shrimp and pat them dry with a paper towel.
3. Place the shrimp on the wooden skewers and then add them in a single layer in the air fryer basket.
4. Air fry the shrimp at 380 degrees Fahrenheit for 8-9 minutes.
5. Carefully remove the shrimp from the air fryer and serve.
6. NOTES
7. Serve shrimp skewers over rice, roasted vegetables, or by themselves with cocktail sauce. You can also serve these air fried shrimp over a salad or for shrimp tacos.
8. You can season the shrimp however you desire. Add a little lemon pepper seasoning, or Old Bay seasoning before cooking. You can also just opt for a little salt and pepper. It's up to you and how you would like to serve them.

Air Fryer Breaded Shrimp
Servings: 4
Cooking Time: 8 Minutes

Ingredients:
- 1 pound large raw shrimp peeled and deveined (I use 31/40 size)
- 1 cup Italian Breadcrumbs
- ¼ cup grated Parmesan cheese
- 1/2 cup all purpose flour
- 1/3 cup water
- 1/2 tsp dried parsley flakes
- 1/2 tsp paprika
- ½ tsp salt
- ¼ tsp ground black pepper
- 1 large egg

Directions:
1. In a shallow bowl, add breadcrumbs, parmesan cheese, parsley flakes, paprika, salt and pepper. Stir with a fork to combine ingredients.
2. In another large bowl, add the flour, egg, and water. Stir together to make a liquid batter.
3. Toss shrimp with the flour and egg batter, until they are coated on both sides.
4. Dredge each piece of shrimp in the panko mixture, coating both sides.
5. Lightly spray the air fryer basket, and place each shrimp into the basket, without stacking or overlapping.
6. Lightly spritz the coated shrimp with olive oil and then place shrimp in the air fryer basket. Air Fry at 380 degrees F for 8-10 minutes, flipping shrimp halfway through air frying.

NOTES

Variations

Use panko breadcrumbs - Instead of using regular bread crumbs, you can use Panko bread crumbs.

Change the seasoning - Use Old Bay seasoning, lemon pepper, red pepper flakes, Cajun seasoning, and any other flavors that you want to add to this shrimp recipe. The flavors take to the larger shrimp easily.

Make air fryer frozen shrimp - If you want to cook tender seafood, you can cook frozen shrimp in the air fryer as well. Just add them in a single layer in the basket of the air fryer.

Air Fryer Fish Tacos

Servings: 3
Cooking Time: 6 Minutes

Ingredients:
- 1 teaspoon garlic powder
- 1 teaspoon chili powder
- 1 teaspoon cumin
- 1/2 teaspoon kosher salt
- 1 cup Panko breadcrumbs
- 1 large egg
- 1 pound fresh cod filets cut in strips or pieces
- 8 small flour or corn tortillas
- Spicy Cream Sauce
- 1/2 cup mayonnaise
- 1/4 cup sriracha sauce
- 1 teaspoon fresh lime juice
- Optional Toppings
- 1 cup purple cabbage shredded
- 1 medium avocado sliced
- 1 cup cotija cheese crumbled
- 1 bunch cilantro garnish

Directions:
1. To prepare the air fryer basket, lightly spray with nonstick cooking spray, then set aside.
2. In a shallow medium bowl, add the garlic powder, chili powder, cumin, salt, and panko breadcrumbs. Stir together until well combined
3. In another shallow bowl, whisk egg. Dip each filet in the whisked egg, and then into the panko breadcrumb mixture. Be sure to coat both sides well.
4. Place filets in a single layer in the prepared air fryer basket and air fry at 350 degrees F for 6-7 minutes until golden brown.

NOTES
Top Tips
I use thinner fish for this recipe. Add a few extra minutes to cooking time if using thicker fish filets.
To confirm doneness, use a fork to flake tilapia fish fillet to see if it easily flakes. To confirm proper temperature, use a meat thermometer to confirm doneness. It should be 130-135 degrees F.
I use fresh tilapia fillets for this simple recipe, but you can use frozen fish fillets as well. Add an additional 2-3 minutes to cooking process.

Air Fryer Tuna Patties

Servings: 10
Cooking Time: 10 Minutes

Ingredients:
- 15 ounces (425 g) canned albacore tuna, drained or 1 pound (454g) fresh tuna, diced
- 2-3 large eggs *see note above
- zest of 1 medium lemon
- 1 Tablespoon (15 ml) lemon juice
- 1/2 cup (55 g) bread crumbs or crushed pork rinds for keto/low carb
- 3 Tablespoons (45 ml) grated parmesan cheese
- 1 stalk celery, finely chopped
- 3 Tablespoons (45 ml) minced onion
- 1/2 teaspoon (2.5 ml) garlic powder
- 1/2 teaspoon (2.5 ml) dried herbs (oregano, dill, basil, thyme or any combo)
- 1/4 teaspoon (1.25 ml) Kosher salt, or to taste
- fresh cracked black pepper
- optional for serving - ranch, tarter sauce, mayo, lemon slices
- EQUIPMENT
- Air Fryer
- Air Fryer Parchment Paper optional
- Perforated Silicone Mats optional
- Oil Sprayer optional

Directions:
1. In a medium bowl, combine the eggs, lemon zest, lemon juice, bread crumbs, parmesan cheese, celery, onion, garlic powder, dried herbs, salt and pepper. Stir to make sure everything is combined. Gently fold in the tuna until just combined.
2. Try to keep all patties same size and thickness for even cooking. Scoop 1/4 cup of mixture, and shape into patties about 3-inches wide x 1/2-inch thick and lay inside basket. Makes about 10 patties.

3. If patties are too soft to handle, chill them for at about 1 hour or until firm. This will make them easier to handle during cooking. Spray or brush top of patties with oil.
4. If you have air fryer perforated baking paper or perforated silicone mats, they are great for this recipe. Lay perforated air fryer baking paper or perforated silicone mat inside base of air fryer. Lightly spray the paper or mat. (if not you don't have the liners, spray enough olive oil spray at the base of the air fryer basket to make sure the patties do not stick)
5. Air Fry at 360°F for 6 minutes. Flip the patties and spray the tops again with oil. Continue to Air Fry for another 3-5 minutes or until cooked to your preference.
6. Serve with your favorite sauce and lemon slices.

NOTES
Easy substitutions: Fresh herbs for the dried herbs. Shallots or green onions for the onions.

Air-fried Beer Battered Fish Tacos With Mango Salsa Recipe

Ingredients:
- For the fish:
- 2 eggs
- 10 ounces of Mexican beer
- 1 1/2 cups of corn starch
- 1 1/2 cups of flour
- 1/2 tablespoon of chili powder
- 1 tablespoon of cumin
- Kosher salt and fresh cracked pepper to taste
- 1 pound of cod cut into large pieces
- Non-stick spray
- For the Salsa & to make the Taco:
- 3 peeled and medium-diced mangos
- 1/2 peeled, seeded and small diced red bell pepper
- 1 peeled, seeded and small diced jalapeno
- 1/2 peeled and small diced red onion
- 1 tablespoon of chopped fresh cilantro
- Juice of 1 lime
- Kosher salt and fresh cracked pepper to taste
- 1/2 thinly sliced head of red cabbage
- Soft corn tortillas
- Crumbled queso fresco for garnish
- Sliced green onions and cilantro leaves for garnish

Directions:
1. For the salsa:
2. Combine the mangos, peppers, onion, chopped cilantro, lime juice together in a medium size bowl and mix. Refrigerate until ready to serve.
3. For the fish:
4. In a medium size bowl whisk together the eggs and beer and set aside.
5. In a separate medium bowl whisk together the cornstarch, flour, chili powder, cumin, salt and pepper.
6. Coat the fish in the egg-beer mixture and transfer it to the flour mixture and dredge to completely coat on all sides.
7. Spray the bottom of the air fryer basket with no-stick spray and place in the fish and spray the tops of the fish with no-stick spray.
8. Cook at 375 degrees for 15 minutes
9. Place the air fried fish on a corn tortilla and top off with cabbage, salsa, queso fresco, green onions, and cilantro.
10. Enjoy!

Air Fryer Calamari

Servings: 4
Cooking Time: 10 Minutes

Ingredients:
- 1/2 cup All purpose flour
- 1 large egg
- 1/3 cup milk regular
- 2 cups panko breadcrumbs
- 1 teaspoon sea salt
- 1 teaspoon ground black pepper
- 1/2 teaspoon paprika
- 1/2 teaspoon garlic powder
- 1 pound calamari rings fresh or frozen
- 1 teaspoon olive oil cooking spray

Directions:
1. Preheat air fryer to 400 degrees F.

2. Create a dredging station with the egg and milk, flour mixture and seasoned breadcrumbs.
3. Place flour in a shallow dish. Set flour aside.
4. In a separate shallow dish whisk the egg and milk together. Set milk mixture aside.
5. In a third separate bowl combine panko, salt, pepper, paprika, and garlic powder together. Set breadcrumb mixture aside.
6. Rinse the calamari with cold water.
7. Then pat the calamari rings dry with a paper towel before dipping to remove excess water.
8. Dip calamari rings in flour (shake off excess flour), then into the egg mixture, and finally in the seasoned panko mixture.
9. Place the calamari rings in a single layer into the air fryer basket. Place extra rings on a baking sheet if working in batches.
10. Spray tops of rings with nonstick cooking spray.
11. Air fry at 400 degrees F for 4 minutes. Flip rings at this point in the cooking process then spray tops with olive oil cooking spray. Continue to air fry for an additional 2-3 minutes or until golden brown and have crispy calamari.
12. If using frozen calamari rings, you may need to add 2-4 minutes of additional cook time. Do not overcook or you will get tough calamari.
13. Place calamari on a wire rack so they remain crispy. Add a sprinkle of salt and black pepper as soon as they are removed from the air fryer.

NOTES
Optional Favorite Dipping Sauce: Cocktail sauce, marinara sauce, tartar sauce, sweet chili sauce, hot sauce, garlic aioli, bechamel sauce or homemade lemon garlic aioli.
Optional Additional Toppings: Lemon wedges, chopped parsley, grated parmesan cheese or fresh lemon juice.Kitchen Tips: You will find fresh or frozen calamari in most local grocery stores.
Substitutions: Use parchment paper for easier clean up. Avocado oil spray instead of olive oil. Use cassava flour or tapioca flour instead of all-purpose flour. Swap out milk for one cup buttermilk.

Air Fryer Salmon And Swiss Chard
Servings: 4
Ingredients:
- 1 medium red onion (sliced 1/2 inch thick)
- 1 1/2 tbsp. oil, divided
- Kosher salt and pepper
- 1 large bunch red Swiss chard (thick stems discarded, leaves chopped)
- 2 cloves garlic (sliced)
- 4 5-oz. salmon fillets
- Chili oil, for serving

Directions:
1. Heat air fryer to 385°F. Toss onion with 1/2 tablespoon oil and a pinch each of salt and pepper and air-fry 5 minutes.
2. Toss with Swiss chard, garlic, 1 tablespoon oil, and 1/4 teaspoon each salt and pepper and air-fry until chard and onion are just tender, about 5 minutes more. Transfer to plates.
3. Season salmon with 1/2 teaspoon each salt and pepper and air-fry at 400°F until skin is crispy and salmon is opaque throughout, 8 to 10 minutes. Serve with chard and drizzle with chili oil if desired.

Air Fryer Bacon Wrapped Shrimp
Servings: 4
Cooking Time: 10 Minutes
Ingredients:
- 24 shrimp
- 1 tbsp Old Bay seasoning
- 8 pieces bacon thinkly sliced, cut into thrids.

Directions:
1. Peel the shrimp and set them aside in a single layer onto a baking sheet.
2. Sprinkle a small amount of Old Bay Seasoning over the peeled shrimp.
3. Cut the bacon pieces into thirds. Carefully wrap the bacon around the shrimp, taking care to tuck the bacon under the bottom of the shrimp.

4. Prepare the basket of the air fryer with olive oil or with a nonstick cooking spray.
5. Add the bacon wrapped shrimp to the basket of the air fryer. Take care to keep the bacon edge tucked under the shrimp.
6. Cook on 390 degrees for 9-10 minutes, or until fully cooked.
7. Carefully remove the shrimp from the air fryer and serve immediately.

NOTES
Bacon wrapped shrimp are delicious all by themselves, but they are also delicious when served with Remoulade sauce, sweet chili sauce, bbq sauce, dijon mustard, or teriyaki sauce.

Air-fryer Fish Tacos
Servings: 4

Ingredients:
- 2 cups shredded green cabbage
- ¼ cup coarsely chopped fresh cilantro
- 1 scallion, thinly sliced
- 5 tablespoons lime juice (from 2 limes), divided
- 1 tablespoon avocado oil
- 1 large avocado
- 2 tablespoons sour cream
- 1 small clove garlic, grated
- ¼ teaspoon salt
- 1 large egg white
- ⅓ cup dry whole-wheat breadcrumbs
- 1 tablespoon chili powder
- 1 pound skinless mahi-mahi fillets, cut into 2- to 3-inch strips
- Avocado oil cooking spray
- 8 (6 inch) corn tortillas, warmed
- 1 medium tomato, chopped

Directions:
1. Toss cabbage, cilantro, scallion, 2 tablespoons lime juice and avocado oil together in a medium bowl; set aside.
2. Cut avocado in half lengthwise; using a spoon, scoop the pulp into the bowl of a mini food processor. Add sour cream, garlic, salt and the remaining 3 tablespoons lime juice; process until smooth, about 30 seconds. (Alternatively, mash with a fork to reach desired consistency.) Set aside.
3. Preheat air fryer to 400°F. Place egg white in a shallow dish; whisk until frothy. Combine breadcrumbs and chili powder in a separate shallow dish. Pat fish dry with a paper towel. Coat the fish with egg white, letting excess drip off; dredge in the breadcrumb mixture, pressing to adhere.
4. Working in batches if needed, arrange the fish in an even layer in the fryer basket; coat the fish well with cooking spray. Cook until crispy and golden on one side, about 3 minutes. Flip the fish; coat with cooking spray and cook until it's crispy and flakes easily, about 3 minutes. Flake the fish into bite-size pieces. Top each tortilla evenly with fish, avocado crema (about 1 tablespoon each), cabbage slaw (about 1/4 cup each) and tomato. Serve with lime wedges, if desired.

Air Fryer Cod
Servings: 4
Cooking Time: 10 Minutes

Ingredients:
- 4 125g Fresh Cod loins: you can substitute for fillets too
- 30 g melted unsalted butter
- 1 Lemon sliced
- Salt to taste
- black pepper to taste

Directions:
1. Preheat the air fryer at 200C/400F for 5 minutes.
2. Pat the cod fillets dry so it is moist-free. Season the fish generously with salt and black pepper then brush the melted butter on one side of the fish
3. Spray the air fryer basket with cooking oil. Place the cod fillet/loin in the air fryer basket buttered side down making sure they are not touching. Brush the remaining butter on top of the fish, add one lemon slice each to the fish
4. Cook for 10 minutes, carefully remove the fish and transfer to a plate. Serve with lemon butter sauce, roasted potatoes and veggies and enjoy!

NOTES
Check on the cod earlier than the time specified for this recipe so as not to overcook the fish. Remember, the thickness of your fish would determine how long it cooks in an air fryer. see the timing on this recipe as a guide. A good starting point to start checking on the fish is from 6 minutes.

As with the majority of air fryer recipes, do not overcrowd the air fryer basket so as to allow the food to cook evenly.

Customise the seasoning to taste.

Let the cod come to room temperature a few minutes before you cook for accurate cooking. The temperature of cooked fish should register at 145F/62C.

Do not leave the fish in the air fryer once the cooking is completed otherwise the fish would overcook and maybe even dry out.

Don't own an air fryer but would like to try this recipe, bake in the oven 200C/400F for 10 minutes. You can also cook your fresh or frozen cod in an air fryer in under 3 minutes.

Air Fryer Blackened Mahi Mahi
Servings: 4
Cooking Time: 9 Minutes

Ingredients:
- 4 mahi mahi fillets 3-4 oz each
- 2 tablespoons olive oil
- 3 tablespoons blackening seasoning

Directions:
1. Preheat air fryer to 400°F.
2. Pat fillets dry and generously rub with olive oil then coat them with blackening seasoning.
3. Place fillets in the air fryer basket and cook for 7-9 minutes.
4. Fish should reach 145°F internally and be opaque and flaky.
5. Notes
6. For the best crispy crust, preheat the air fryer first. If cooking in batches, keep warm in the oven and broil before serving.
7. Cooking time can vary with the thickness of the fish. Check the temperature of the fish early to ensure it doesn't overcook.
8. Serving Suggestion: Serve with fruit salsa like pineapple salsa or the quick bell pepper salsa below.
9. Quick Bell Pepper Salsa (optional): Dice one Roma tomato, half a bell pepper, and two tablespoons of red onion. Season with a squeeze of lime juice, a teaspoon of olive oil, and salt and pepper. Add a sprinkle of cilantro.

Air Fryer Salmon With Maple Soy Glaze
Servings: 4
Cooking Time: 8 Minutes

Ingredients:
- 3 tbsp pure maple syrup
- 3 tbsp reduced sodium soy sauce (or gluten-free soy sauce)
- 1 tbsp sriracha hot sauce
- 1 clove garlic (smashed)
- 4 wild salmon fillets (skinless (6 oz each))

Directions:
1. Combine maple syrup, soy sauce, sriracha and garlic in a small bowl, pour into a gallon sized resealable bag and add the salmon.
2. Marinate 20 to 30 minutes, turning once in a while.
3. Lightly spray the basket with oil.
4. Remove the fish from the marinade, reserving and pat dry with paper towels.
5. Place the fish in the air fryer, in batches, air fry 400F 7 to 8 minutes, or longer depending on thickness of the salmon.
6. Meanwhile, pour the marinade in a small saucepan and bring to a simmer over medium-low heat and reduce until it thickens into a glaze, 1 to 2 minutes. Spoon over salmon just before eating.

POULTRY RECIPES

Chicken Sausage In The Air Fryer

Servings: 5
Cooking Time: 10 Minutes

Ingredients:
- 5 Apple Chicken Sausages

Directions:
1. Preheat your air fryer to 370 degrees F. Place your chicken sausages in the air fryer, spaced apart. Cook for 8 to 10 minutes.
2. At the halfway point, flip the sausages. If you want, you can spray the sausages with some cooking spray to help them look crispier.
3. Serve and enjoy!

NOTES
HOW TO REHEAT CHICKEN SAUSAGES IN THE AIR FRYER:
Place the links in your air fryer at 350 degrees F. Cook for 3 to 4 minutes, or until heated through.
HOW TO COOK FROZEN CHICKEN SAUSAGE IN THE AIR FRYER
Preheat your air fryer to 350 degrees F.
Place the frozen chicken sausage in the air fryer in a single layer with space between each link. Cook for 11 to 13 minutes, flipping halfway through.

How To Reheat Fried Chicken

Cooking Time: 10 Minutes

Ingredients:
- 6 pieces fried chicken
- salt and pepper optional

Directions:
1. Preheat the air fryer to 350°F.
2. Place the chicken in the air fryer basket and cook for 5 minutes.
3. Flip the chicken and cook for another 5 minutes or until crispy.
4. Season with salt and pepper if desired.

Frozen Chicken Thighs In The Air Fryer

Servings: 4-6
Cooking Time: 30 Minutes

Ingredients:
- 1 1/2 to 2 pounds frozen chicken thighs
- 1 tablespoon McCormick Lemon Pepper Seasoning

Directions:
1. Preheat your air fryer to 380 degrees F.
2. Place separated frozen chicken thighs in the air fryer and cook for 15 minutes until the chicken is just thawed.
3. Remove the chicken from the basket.
4. Spray each thigh with cooking oil, then sprinkle on the lemon pepper seasoning evenly.
5. Return the chicken to the basket and cook for 12-15 additional minutes, flipping once halfway through.
6. Remove the chicken thighs from the air fryer and enjoy with your favorite sides.

NOTES
HOW TO REHEAT CHICKEN THIGHS IN THE AIR FRYER
Preheat the air fryer to 350 degrees F.
Place the leftover chicken thighs in the air fryer. Cook for 3 to 5 minutes until heated through.
How to Cook Thawed Chicken Thighs in the Air Fryer:
Preheat your air fryer to 380 degrees.
Coat the chicken thighs evenly with Lemon Pepper seasoning then place in the air fryer in a single layer.
Cook for 12 to 15 minutes until chicken reaches 165 degrees.

Air Fryer Frozen Turkey Burgers

Servings: 4
Cooking Time: 15 Minutes

Ingredients:
- 4 frozen turkey burgers ½ inch thick
- 4 tablespoons barbecue sauce
- For Serving
- 4 hamburger buns
- lettuce, tomatoes, onions, mayonnaise optional

Directions:
1. Preheat air fryer to 375°F.

2. Place turkey burgers in a single layer in the air fryer basket.
3. Cook burgers for 13-14 minutes, flipping halfway through the cook time and brushing with bbq sauce.
4. Serve on hamburger buns with desired fixings.

Air-fryer Crispy Salt And Pepper Chicken Wings Recipe

Servings: 4
Cooking Time: 20 Minutes

Ingredients:
- 1kg-1.2kg pack Willow Farm chicken wings (about 16 wings)1kg-1.2kg pack Willow Farm Chicken wings (about 16 wings)
- 1 tsp sesame oil
- 1 tsp Shaoxing rice wine or Japanese mirin
- 30g plain flour
- ½ tsp white pepper
- ¼ tsp ground ginger
- sunflower oil spray
- 1 red chilli, thinly sliced
- 2-3 cloves of garlic, chopped
- 2 spring onions, thinly sliced
- For the dipping sauce
- 4 tbsp light mayo
- 100g natural yogurt
- 1 tbsp rice vinegar
- 1 tsp light soy sauce
- 1 tbsp caster sugar
- 2 tsp mild curry powder

Directions:
1. Preheat the air-fryer to 180°C.
2. In a large bowl, toss the chicken wings with the sesame oil and rice wine or mirin. Sprinkle over the flour, the white pepper, ground ginger, and some salt and black pepper, tossing until evenly coated.
3. Working in 2 batches, spray the basket of the air-fryer with a little oil and arrange half the chicken wings in a single layer with some space between them. Spray with oil and cook for 10 mins.
4. Tip into clean bowl and cook the next batch.
5. Put the sliced chilli, garlic and spring onion into the bowl with both batches of part-cooked chicken wings and shake to coat. Add everything from the bowl back into the air-fryer and cook for 10-15 mins, until dark golden brown and cooked through.
6. Meanwhile, stir together the ingredients for the dipping sauce, cover and chill for 10 mins before serving with the cooked chicken wings.

Air Fryer Chicken Cordon Bleu

Servings: 4
Cooking Time: 20 Minutes

Ingredients:
- 4 small chicken breasts boneless skinless, 4-5 oz each
- salt and ground black pepper to taste
- ⅛ teaspoon dried thyme leaves
- 4 slices deli Swiss cheese
- 4 slices deli ham
- 1 egg beaten
- ⅓ cup panko bread crumbs
- ½ cup seasoned bread crumbs

Directions:
1. Place the chicken breast on a flat work surface and butterfly the chicken by cutting most of the way through so it opens like a book. Pound to ¼ " thickness.
2. Season chicken with salt, pepper, and thyme.
3. Place the ham and cheese inside each chicken breast. Close the breasts and secure with a toothpick.
4. Mix panko bread crumbs and seasoned bread crumbs in a shallow dish. Dip chicken into egg and then bread crumbs.
5. Preheat the air fryer to 370°F.
6. Generously spray the rolls with cooking spray and place in the bottom of the air fryer basket.
7. Cook 10 minutes. Flip chicken over and cook an additional 8-10 minutes or until bread crumbs are crisp and chicken reaches 165°F.

Asian Glazed Crispy Chicken Thighs

Ingredients:
- 4 pieces of chicken thighs
- 1/3 cup Soy Sauce
- 1/3 Cup Hoisin Sauce
- 2 T Sesame oil
- 2 T Olive oil
- 2 T Chilli oil
- 2 T Honey
- 2 cloves fresh garlic - crushed
- 3cm fresh ginger - crushed
- 1 T smoked Chilli flakes
- Salt & Pepper
- Fresh Spring onion for garnish

Directions:
1. Mix all the ingredients together to form a marinade for the chicken. Place in the refrigerator for minimum 30min.
2. Once marinaded - preheat Instant Pot Air Fryer to 205C on Bake setting. Place the thighs in the basket and retain the leftover sauce in the bowl. Bake for 25min - turning halfway.
3. Heat the remaining sauce in a saucepan over medium high heat until it slightly thickens. Drizzle sauce over the cooked chicken and garnish with the fresh spring onion. Enjoy!!

Air Fryer Turkey Meatballs

Servings: 4
Cooking Time: 12 Minutes

Ingredients:
- 1 pound ground turkey
- 1 egg
- 1 teaspoon Italian seasoning
- 2 teaspoons Worcestershire sauce
- 2 tablespoons grated onion
- ¼ teaspoon salt
- ½ cup seasoned bread crumbs
- ¼ cup grated parmesan cheese

Directions:
1. Preheat air fryer to 350°F.
2. Mix all ingredients in a large bowl.
3. Divide into 16 meatballs and place in a single layer in the air fryer basket.
4. Cook for 12-14 minutes or just until meatballs reach 165°F. (Do not overcook)

Air Fryer Nashville Hot Chicken Hack

Servings: 2
Cooking Time: 20 Minutes

Ingredients:
- FOR THE CHICKEN:
- About 2-4 frozen pre-cooked breaded chicken breasts
- FOR THE NASHVILLE HOT SAUCE:
- 1/4 cup (60 g) butter
- 1/4 cup (60 ml) oil
- 1 Tablespoon (15 ml) ground cayenne pepper, or 2 Tablespoons for extra hot
- 2 Tablespoons (30 ml) brown sugar
- 1 teaspoon (5 ml) garlic powder
- 1 teaspoon (5 ml) paprika
- 1 Tablespoon (15 ml) Worcestershire sauce or soy sauce
- 1/2 teaspoon (2.5 ml) salt, or to taste
- 1 teaspoon (5 ml) black pepper
- FOR SERVING
- 6-8 slices (6-8 slices) white bread
- Pickles, whatever you prefer - bread & butter, dill, or both
- EQUIPMENT
- Air Fryer

Directions:
1. Make the Sauce: Combine all the sauce ingredients in a bowl or saucepan (butter, oil, cayenne pepper, brown sugar, garlic powder, paprika, Worcestershire or soy sauce, salt and pepper). Microwave or heat until butter is just melted (the hotter it is, the harder it will be to emulsify the spices in the liquids). Whisk thoroughly until smooth.
2. When the sauce is cooler, it doesn't separate as easily so we like to brush sauce on the chicken when the sauce is slightly cooler or room temperature. If you want your sauce warmer, then keep stirring or whisking the sauce as you brush the chicken so that you have as little separation of sauce/oil as possible. The warmer the sauce is, the more the spices will want to separate from the liquids.
3. Place the frozen breaded chicken breasts in the air fryer basket in a single layer. Make

sure they aren't overlapping. No oil spray is needed.
4. Air Fry at 380°F/193°C for 10 minutes. Flip the chicken over.
5. Continue to Air Fry at 380°F/193°C for another 2 minutes. Check the chicken breasts and if needed, add another 2-3 minutes or until heated through and crispy to your preference.
6. Place chicken on top of white bread. Brush both sides of chicken with the hot sauce. Top with pickles and serve warm. Enjoy!

NOTES
Air Frying Tips and Notes:
No Oil Necessary. Cook Frozen - Do not thaw first.
Don't overcrowd the air fryer basket. Lay in a single layer.
Recipe timing is based on a non-preheated air fryer. If cooking in multiple batches of chicken back to back, the following batches may cook a little quicker.
Recipes were tested in 3.7 to 6 qt. air fryers. If using a larger air fryer, the chicken might cook quicker so adjust cooking time.
Remember to set a timer to flip/toss as directed in recipe.

Air Fryer Fried Chicken

Servings: 3

Ingredients:
- 2 lb. skin-on, bone-in chicken pieces (a mix of cuts)
- 2 c. buttermilk
- 1/2 c. hot sauce
- 3 tsp. kosher salt, divided
- 2 c. all-purpose flour
- 1 tsp. garlic powder
- 1 tsp. onion powder
- 1/2 tsp. dried oregano
- 1/2 tsp. freshly ground black pepper
- 1/4 tsp. cayenne pepper

Directions:
1. Trim chicken of any excess fat and transfer to a large bowl. In a medium bowl, combine buttermilk, hot sauce, and 2 teaspoons salt. Pour buttermilk mixture over chicken, making sure all pieces are coated. Cover bowl and refrigerate at least 1 hour or up to overnight.
2. In a shallow bowl or pie dish, combine flour, garlic powder, onion powder, oregano, black pepper, cayenne, and remaining 1 teaspoon salt. Working one at a time, remove chicken from buttermilk mixture, shaking off any excess. Place in flour mixture, turning to coat.
3. Working in batches if necessary, in an air-fryer basket, arrange chicken (do not overcrowd). Cook at 400°, turning halfway through, until chicken is golden brown and an instant-read thermometer inserted into thickest part registers 165°, 20 to 25 minutes.

Air Fryer Bacon Wrapped Chicken Bites

Servings: 4
Cooking Time: 10 Minutes

Ingredients:
- 1 pound boneless, skinless chicken breast
- 1 teaspoon olive oil
- 1/4 teaspoon smoked paprika
- 1/4 teaspoon garlic powder
- 1 Tablespoon brown sugar
- 6 slices bacon
- 2 Tablespoons Barbecue sauce

Directions:
1. Preheat the air fryer to 390 degrees Fahrenheit. Prepare the air fryer basket with nonstick cooking oil if needed.
2. Cut the raw chicken breasts into bite sized pieces.
3. Add the paprika, brown sugar, and garlic powder in a small bowl and mix until combined. Set aside.
4. Coat the chicken bites in olive oil and then toss the chicken pieces in the brown sugar mixture.
5. Take each slice of bacon and cut the bacon strips in half to fit the chicken bites.
6. Wrap each of the seasoned chicken bites with a piece of bacon.

7. Place each bacon wrapped piece of chicken in a single layer in the air fryer basket. Cook at 390 degrees Fahrenheit for 8-9 minutes, or until you have crispy bacon and the internal temperature has reached 165 degrees Fahrenheit.
8. Carefully remove the chicken bites from the Air Fryer and serve with your favorite dipping sauce such as barbecue sauce.

NOTES

What if I don't have chicken breasts? Can I use a different cut of chicken?
Absolutely! If you don't have boneless skinless chicken breasts, consider using boneless skinless chicken thighs, chicken strips, or chicken tenderloins.
Can I substitute the seasonings with this chicken bites recipe?
Yes! Consider using different seasonings such as cayenne pepper, chili powder, black pepper, or your favorite seasonings.
How do I store leftover bacon chicken bites?
Store leftover bacon wrapped chicken bites in an airtight container in the refrigerator for up to 3 days. To reheat, place the bacon wrapped chicken bites back into the air fryer and cook at 390 degrees Fahrenheit for 2-3 minutes or until heated through.

Air Fryer Turkey Breast

Servings: 10
Cooking Time: 55 Minutes

Ingredients:
- 4 pound turkey breast (on the bone with skin (ribs removed))
- 1 tablespoon olive oil
- 2 teaspoons kosher
- 1/2 tablespoon dry turkey or poultry seasoning (I used Bell's which has not salt)

Directions:
1. Rub 1/2 tablespoon of oil all over the turkey breast. Season both sides with salt and turkey seasoning then rub in the remaining half tablespoon of oil over the skin side.
2. Preheat the air fryer 350F and cook skin side down 20 minutes, turn over and cook until the internal temperature is 160F using an instant-read thermometer about 30 to 40 minutes more depending on the size of your breast. Let is rest 10 minutes before carving.
3. Notes
4. Without the skin the smart points will be 0.

Air Fryer Tandoori Turkey Breast

Servings: 4

Ingredients:
- 1 split skin-on, bone-in turkey breast (about 1 3/4 lb.)
- 1 1/2 tsp. kosher salt, divided
- 1 c. full-fat plain Greek yogurt
- 2 cloves garlic, minced
- 1 tbsp. sweet paprika
- 2 tsp. ground turmeric
- 2 tsp. minced fresh ginger (from a 1" piece)
- 1 tsp. ground cumin
- Olive oil cooking spray

Directions:
1. Pat turkey dry with paper towels; season all over with 1 teaspoon salt.
2. In a medium bowl, combine yogurt, garlic, paprika, turmeric, ginger, cumin, and remaining 1/2 teaspoon salt. Spread yogurt mixture all over turkey. Let stand at room temperature for 30 minutes.
3. Lightly coat an air-fryer basket with cooking spray. Place turkey in basket. Cook at 350°, flipping every 10 minutes, until turkey is golden brown and an instant-read thermometer inserted into thickest part of breast registers 165°, 35 to 40 minutes. Let turkey rest about 10 minutes before slicing.

Butter Chicken

Servings: 6
Cooking Time: 30 Minutes

Ingredients:
- 1 ½ pounds boneless, skinless chicken breast, cut into 1-inch pieces
- Kosher salt, as needed
- 3 tablespoons ghee
- ½ cup shallots, thinly sliced

- 1 can fire roasted crushed tomatoes (28 ounces)
- 1 ½ tablespoons fresh ginger, grated
- 6 garlic cloves, minced
- 1 tablespoons ground fenugreek
- 2 ½ teaspoons kosher salt, plus more as needed
- 2 teaspoon ground paprika
- 2 teaspoons turmeric
- 1 teaspoon ground cumin
- ½ teaspoon ground cardamom
- ¼ teaspoon ground cloves
- 1/3 cup cashew butter
- 1 cup chicken stock
- 1 can coconut milk (15 ounces)
- 2 tablespoons fresh cilantro, chopped, for serving
- Warm naan bread, for serving
- Items Needed:
- Blender

Directions:
1. Season the chicken generously with kosher salt.
2. Select the Sauté Function on the Pressure Cooker and press Temp Set, then customize the temperature to high and time to 12 minutes.
3. Add 2 tablespoons of ghee into the pressure cooker, then sear off the chicken in batches, removing the chicken to a plate as each piece is golden brown on all sides.
4. Add the remaining ghee and the shallots into the inner pot and cook, stirring occasionally, until the shallots are translucent, then stir in the garlic, ginger, and spices, followed by the cashew butter. Pour in the tomatoes and chicken stock stir to dissolve the cashew butter, then add the chicken pieces back into the pot.
5. Place the lid onto the pressure cooker.
6. Select the Pressure function, adjust pressure to high, and time to 15 minutes, then press Start.
7. Slowly release pressure by sliding the vent switch in between Seal and Vent. Slide the switch to Vent after 15 minutes.
8. Open the lid carefully.
9. Stir the coconut milk into the sauce, then adjust the seasoning to taste with kosher salt.
10. Serve the butter chicken on plates with naan, garnished with cilantro.

Air Fryer Chicken Tenders With Flour
Servings: 4
Cooking Time: 40 Minutes

Ingredients:
- 1 pound chicken tenders
- ½ cup buttermilk (optional, for marinating)
- ½ cup all-purpose flour
- ½ teaspoon paprika
- ½ teaspoon garlic powder
- ½ teaspoon salt
- ½ teaspoon black pepper
- ¼ teaspoon baking powder
- 1 large egg
- 1 teaspoon water

Directions:
1. Marinating (optional): Place chicken tenders in a plastic zipper bag with the buttermilk and marinate in the refrigerator for at least 30 minutes, up to 2 hours.
2. When ready to cook, remove the chicken from the fridge and allow it to sit at room temperature for 15 minutes.
3. Meanwhile, whisk together the egg and water in a large bowl until well combined. Transfer the chicken tenders to the bowl, then discard the marinade and bag.
4. Preheat the air fryer to 370 degrees F.
5. In a clean plastic zipper bag, add the flour, paprika, garlic powder, salt, pepper, and baking powder. Seal and shake well to combine.
6. Working in batches of 3 to 4 at a time, remove the tenders from the egg, allowing excess to drop off, then place them in the bag with the flour. Seal and shake the bag to evenly coat the chicken. Remove the tenders to a plate, shaking off any excess flour, and repeat with the remaining pieces.
7. Lay the tenders in an even layer in the air fryer basket, working in batches as needed,

so you don't overcrowd them. Generously spray the tenders with cooking spray until the flour appears damp.
8. Air fry the tenders for 15-20 minutes, flipping them once halfway through and spritzing them again with cooking spray. Continue cooking until the tenders are golden and 165 degrees F internally. (Exact cooking time will vary depending on the size of your tenders, your air fryer, etc.).

Air Fryer Chicken Nuggets
Servings: 4
Cooking Time: 10 Minutes

Ingredients:
- 1 lb boneless skinless chicken breast
- 1/2 tsp salt
- 1/4 tsp pepper
- 1/4 cup flour
- 1/2 cup melted butter or 1 large egg
- 1/2 cup breadcrumbs
- 1/2 cup parmesan grated
- 1 tsp dried parsley
- olive oil spray
- Garnish:
- ketchup, bbq sauce, ranch dressing, or your favorite dipping sauce.

Directions:
1. Trim any excess fat from the chicken breast and cut the chicken into nugget-sized pieces. Season with salt and pepper.
2. Set out 3 shallow bowls. In the first bowl put the flour, in the second bowl put the melted butter or beaten egg.
3. In the third bowl, mix together the breadcrumbs, dried parsley, and parmesan cheese.
4. One at a time dip each piece of chicken in the flour first, then the butter or egg, and finally the breadcrumb mixture.
5. Once all nuggets are ready to cook, give them a light spray with olive oil and place them on a single layer in the air fryer. Cook for 7 minutes at 400F and then flip the nuggets. Cook for another 1 to 3 minutes at 400F until they are golden.
6. Serve with your favorite dipping sauce.

Notes
Make sure not to overcrowd the air fryer basket. The hot air needs to reach all the sides of the nuggets, so they crisp up.
Press the breadcrumbs onto the nuggets to help them adhere well. Doing so helps give the chicken a more even coating.
The key to cooking chicken nuggets in the air fryer perfectly is to ensure all the chicken nuggets are as uniformly as possible. You want them all to cook for the same amount of time.
After dipping the chicken nuggets, shake off any excess egg so the nuggets don't taste eggy.

Chicken Parmesan With Quick Garlic Pull-apart Rolls
Servings: 4
Cooking Time: 20 Minutes

Ingredients:
- Quick Garlic Pull-apart Rolls
- 3 cups self-raising flour
- 1 cup full cream plain yoghurt
- 1/2 cup melted butter
- 4 cloves garlic, crushed
- 1/2 Tbsp chopped parsley
- Pinch of salt
- 2 chicken breasts, halved lengthways
- 1/3 cup flour
- 1/2 tsp each onion powder and paprika
- 2 large eggs, whisked
- 1 cup breadcrumbs
- 1/4 cup freshly grated Parmesan cheese
- 1 tsp dried oregano
- salt and pepper to taste
- Cheats Marinara sauce
- 1 cup tinned chopped tomatoes
- 1 Tbsp olive oil
- 1 garlic clove, crushed
- 1/2 tsp each salt and dried basil
- 1/4 tsp ground pepper
- 1 cup grated mozzarella
- fresh basil, for garnish

Directions:
1. Start with the quick rolls: combine the flour, salt and yoghurt in a medium bowl and knead for 7-8 minutes until a smooth dough is formed. Cut into 8 balls and place

in a greased dish that fits the Vortex Dual drawer. Cover with a cloth while the drawer heats to the correct temperature.
2. Prepare the coating sequence: place flour, onion powder and paprika in a shallow bowl. Place eggs in a second bowl and in a third combine breadcrumbs, Parmesan and dried oregano.
3. Turn on the Vortex Dual and set drawer 1 to Air Fry 180C for 12 minutes and drawer 2 to Bake at 180C for 20 minutes. Press Sync Finish and Start to commence preheating.
4. Season the chicken breast fillets on both sides. Coat one fillet at a time in the flour mix, then eggs and lastly toss in the breadcrumbs and press gently to ensure the crumbs are well adhered.
5. Add all 4 crumbed fillets to drawer 1 and cook for 7 minutes, turn half way through the cook time.
6. Add the rolls to drawer 2 to Bake.
7. For the cheats marinara, combine the ingredients in a medium bowl and use a fork to mash the tomato chunks and mix all the ingredients.
8. With 5 minutes left, open the drawer and top the crumbed chicken fillets with the sauce and grated mozzarella allow to cook until the cheese is melted.
9. Combine the melted butter, garlic and parsley in a small bowl and when the rolls are 5 minutes from the end brush over the top.
10. When all the cooking has ended, remove the chicken fillets and garlic rolls, brush over more garlic and herb butter and serve with a leafy side salad and garnished with basil.

Air Fryer Chicken Fried Steak

Servings: 4
Cooking Time: 15 Minutes

Ingredients:
- 4 cube steaks
- 1 1/2 cups all purpose flour
- 1 egg
- 2 teaspoons baking powder
- 1/2 teaspoon paprika
- 1 teaspoon ground black pepper
- 1/2 teaspoon onion powder
- 1/2 teaspoon garlic powder
- 1/2 teaspoon white pepper
- 1 Tablespoon hot sauce
- 1 cup milk

Directions:
1. Combine the flour, paprika, salt, black pepper, white pepper, garlic powder, onion powder, and baking powder in a large shallow bowl. Whisk together and set aside.
2. Combine the milk, egg, and hot sauce in a second bowl. Mix well.
3. Take the fresh cube steaks and dip them into the dry mixture, the egg mixture, and then back into the flour mixture.
4. Repeat this with your cube steaks and place them on a baking sheet.
5. Spray both sides of the prepared cube steaks with a few spritzes of oil cooking spray.
6. Prepare the Air Fryer basket with olive oil cooking spray or perforated parchment paper.
7. Place the cube steaks in a single layer in the air fryer basket and cook at 400°F. for 8 minutes.
8. Use a spatula to flip each steak carefully, spray once more with olive oil spray, and cook for another 5-6 minutes until the tops are golden brown with a crispy coating.
9. Serve with white gravy, green beans, corn, cornbread, or any of your favorite side dishes.

NOTES
This recipe was made using a 5.8 qt basket style Cosori Air Fryer. If you are using a different type of air fryer, you may need to adjust the cooking time with this recipe. Some air fryers can cook a little faster, and some can cook much slower, This air fryer is 5.8 qt with a power output of 1700 watts. If you are using an air fryer that is larger or using less power, you will need to increase the cooking time.

Make sure you don't overcrowd your steaks in the Air Fryer, or they won't cook evenly. The steaks can touch as long as they aren't on top of one another.

Excess flour causes the steaks to become too bready, so make sure you tap off extra flour before placing your steaks in the Air Fryer.

Cube steaks are best for this recipe because they are already tenderized and pre-cut when you buy them. Cube steaks are incredibly tender, making them perfect for this recipe. If you can't find cubed steak at your local grocery store, you can make cube steaks yourself by buying a sirloin, tenderizing it with a meat tenderizer, and making small cube-like cuts in the meat.

Air Fryer Chicken Wings

Servings: 10
Cooking Time: 30 Minutes

Ingredients:
- FOR THE WINGS:
- 1 1/2 pounds chicken wings
- 1 teaspoon kosher salt
- 2 tablespoons unsalted butter
- 1/4 cup hot sauce Frank's RedHot is what I use
- 1 tablespoon minced garlic
- 1/2 tablespoon white vinegar
- Nonstick cooking spray
- TO SERVE:
- Blue cheese sauce The Well Plated Cookbook, page 212 or blue cheese dressing of choice
- Celery sticks
- Chopped fresh chives optional for color

Directions:
1. Coat the basket of a 3 quart or larger air fryer with nonstick spray.
2. Trim off the wing tips (you should be able to feel the joint soft spot). It should separate fairly easily, but if not, put the blade in place, then carefully but firmly hit the top of your knife to apply extra pressure. Discard. Next, split the drumette side of each wing from the flat side at the joint: slice down through the skin feeling for the "soft spot" and wiggle your knife as needed.
3. Pat the wings very dry. Sprinkle all over with salt.
4. Place the wings in the air fryer in a single layer, making sure they do not touch (if needed, stand up the drumettes along the side). Set the air fryer to 360 degrees F. Cook the wings for 12 minutes, then remove the basket and with tongs, flip the wings over. Return to the air fryer at 360 degrees for 12 additional minutes.
5. Slide out the basket, flip the wings once more, then return them to the air fryer. Increase the air fryer temperature to 390 degrees F. Cook the wings for 6 minutes, flipping once more halfway through. The skin should look nice and crisp (if your wings are on the larger side, they may need a few more minutes).
6. While the wings finish up, melt the butter in a large microwave safe bowl in the microwave or a saucepan on the stove. Stir in the hot sauce, garlic, and vinegar until smooth.
7. Transfer the wings to the bowl with the hot sauce mixture. Toss to throughly coat the wings. Transfer the wings to a serving plate. Sprinkle with chives as desired. Enjoy warm with blue cheese sauce and celery.

Notes

TO MAKE IN THE OVEN: Place a broiler rack 4 to 6 inches from the broiler. Preheat to high. Line a rimmed baking sheet with foil and place an oven safe baking rack on top. Arrange the wings on the rack in a single layer so they do not touch. Broil for 20 to 25 minutes, until the wings are browned and crisp, flipping once halfway through.

TO STORE. Refrigerate leftover chicken wings for up to 3 days.

TO REHEAT. Let the wings come to room temperature. Mist with water to help make them juicy, then reheat in the oven at 350 degrees F for 10 to 12 minutes, or the air fryer at 350 degrees F for 6 minutes, turning once halfway through.

Air Fryer Crumbed Chicken Schnitzel

Servings: 4
Cooking Time: 35 Minutes

Ingredients:
- 8 Coles RSPCA Approved Australian Chicken Thigh Fillets
- 1 cup (80g) panko breadcrumbs
- 45g pkt lemon and herb dukkah
- 2 Coles Australian Free Range Eggs, lightly whisked
- 1/3 cup (50g) plain flour
- 350g pkt Coles Kaleslaw Kit
- Select all ingredients

Directions:
1. Place half the chicken between 2 sheets of plastic wrap. Use a meat mallet or rolling pin to gently pound until 2cm thick. Repeat with the remaining chicken.
2. Combine the breadcrumbs and dukkah in a shallow bowl. Place the egg in a medium bowl. Place the flour on a plate and season. Coat each piece of chicken in flour, shaking off excess. Dip in egg, then in breadcrumb mixture and turn to coat. Transfer to a plate. Cover with plastic wrap and place in the fridge for 30 mins to rest.
3. Preheat air fryer to 200°C. Spray the chicken with olive oil spray. Arrange half the chicken in a single layer in the basket of the air fryer. Cook, turning halfway through cooking, for 16 mins or until golden and cooked through. Transfer to a plate and cover with foil to keep warm. Repeat with remaining chicken.
4. Meanwhile, prepare the kaleslaw kit in a bowl following packet directions.
5. Divide the chicken and kaleslaw among serving plates. Season.

RECIPE NOTES
Allow for 30 minutes chilling time.
SERVE WITH lemon wedges.
On the stove: To make this without an air fryer, cook the chicken in 1cm of olive oil in a large frying pan over medium-high heat for 4-5 mins each side or until cooked through.

Air Fryer Chili Crisp Crunch Chicken Wings

Servings: 4
Cooking Time: 30 Minutes

Ingredients:
- 2 pounds (907 g) chicken wings
- Kosher salt , or sea salt, to taste
- black pepper , to taste
- garlic powder , optional
- 1/4 cup chili crisp crunch , or to taste
- OPTIONAL - FOR EXTRA CRISPY CORN STARCH CRUST
- 1/4 cup (30 g) corn starch , or as needed
- oil spray , as needed
- EQUIPMENT
- Air Fryer
- Oil Sprayer optional

Directions:
1. If you have whole wings, separate them into the drum and flat. If needed, pat dry the chicken wings. Season with salt, pepper, and optional garlic powder.
2. For oil-free version, place in even layer in air fryer basket/tray. Follow air fry instructions below. For Extra Crispy Crust, follow optional steps for corn starch crust.
3. FOR EXTRA CRISPY CORN STARCH CRUST
4. Add seasoning to the wings then lay them in single layer on a plate or cutting board. Sprinkle cornstarch over the wings on both sides.
5. Liberally spray wings evenly with oil spray so that all the cornstarch is coated in oil. There should be no dry white clumps of cornstarch or else they will cook hard and dry.
6. Place the coated wings in your air fryer basket or tray/rack.
7. AIR FRY
8. Air Fry wings at 400°F/205°C for 20 minutes minutes or until crispy-looking and nearly cooked through.
9. Flip the wings and Air Fry at 400°F/205°C for additional 5-10 minutes or until wings are fully cooked and crispy.
10. Toss with the chili crisp/crunch to taste. Spiciness will vary greatly on the brand of

chili crisp/crunch, as well has how much you use on the wings. Adjust to your preference.

NOTES

No Oil Necessary. The wings have enough fat in the skin to crisp up nicely on their own.

Shake several times for even cooking.

Don't overcrowd fryer basket.

If using a sauce, it is added in just at the end, otherwise it often burns before the chicken wings are cooked.

Recipes were cooked in 3-4 qt air fryers. If using a larger air fryer, the recipe might cook quicker so adjust cooking time.

If cooking in multiple batches, the first batch will take longer to cook if Air Fryer is not already pre-heated.

Remember to set a timer to shake/flip/toss the food as directed in recipe.

Crispy Air Fryer Fried Chicken Breast

Servings: 4
Cooking Time: 10 Minutes

Ingredients:
- 2 boneless skinless chicken breasts sliced into thin cutlets
- 1 Tablespoon olive oil
- ½ cup panko bread crumbs
- ½ cup dried bread crumbs
- ¼ teaspoon cayenne pepper
- ½ teaspoon garlic powder
- 1/2 teaspoon onion powder
- ½ teaspoon ground black pepper
- ½ teaspoon white pepper
- 1 teaspoon olive oil spray

Directions:
1. Coat both sides of the chicken with an even coating of olive oil.
2. In a rimmed dish, combine the bread crumbs, panko, and seasonings.
3. Coat each piece of chicken with the seasoned bread crumbs. Spray each breaded chicken breast with a light coat of olive oil.
4. Place the chicken breasts into a single layer into the air fryer basket.
5. Air fry chicken at 390 degrees Fahreheit for 10-12 minutes, flipping the chicken halfway through the cooking time.
6. Carefully remove the chicken from the air fryer and serve immediately.

NOTES

Use a different cut of chicken - This recipe can be made with chicken thighs, chicken drumsticks, and any other chicken pieces that you want.

Add brown sugar - If you want to make the boneless skinless chicken breast a little sweet, adding a little sugar will be perfect.

Spice things up by adding a little chili powder.

For extra crispy chicken, soak the chicken in a buttermilk mixture with egg for about 30 minutes to an hour before breading. Add a light coat of flour mixture before dipping it into egg and then seasoned breadcrumbs. Spray with olive oil before air frying.

How to make Unbreaded Fried Chicken in the Air Fryer

Coat both sides of the chicken with an even coating of olive oil.

In a rimmed dish or shallow bowl, combine the seasonings.

Coat each piece of chicken with the seasonings. Once seasoned, spray each breaded chicken breast with a light coat of olive oil.

Place the chicken breasts into a single layer into the air fryer basket.

Air fry chicken at 390 degrees Fahrenheit for 10-12 minutes, flipping the chicken halfway through the cooking time.

Carefully remove the chicken from the air fryer and serve immediately.

Air Fryer Doritos Crusted Chicken Strips

Servings: 6
Cooking Time: 25 Minutes

Ingredients:
- 9 oz. (255 g) Doritos or any flavor tortilla chips
- 1 large egg , beaten (or more if needed)
- 2 pounds (907 g) chicken , cut into thin strips

- 1 teaspoon (5 ml) garlic powder
- 1/2 teaspoon (2.5 ml) salt
- fresh black pepper, to taste
- For dipping: Ranch, sour cream, ketchup, bbq sauce or your favorite sauce
- EQUIPMENT
- Air Fryer

Directions:
1. Crush the Doritos or tortilla chips in a bag with a rolling pin. Crush them thoroughly. The smaller the pieces, the better they'll coat the chicken. Place the crushed chips in a bowl for dredging the chicken. Put the beaten egg in another bowl.
2. Season the chicken strips with garlic powder, salt and pepper.
3. Working with one or two chicken strips at a time, first coat the chicken strips with the egg, then coat with the crushed Doritos. Gently press the chicken into the crushed chips, then pour chip pieces over the chicken strips. Gently press chips into chicken. This help chips to stay dry. If they're wet, they stick less to the chicken.
4. Pre-heat your Air Fryer at 380°F (195°C) for 4 minutes. Spray the air fryer basket or racks with oil spray. Gently lay chicken pieces in the basket or on the racks in a single layer (cook in batches if needed). Spray oil spray on top of coated chicken.
5. Air Fry at 380°F (195°C) for 15 minutes. Gently turn the chicken pieces and spray the tops with oil spray (make sure to turn the chicken gently or else the chip pieces will fall off).
6. Air Fry for additional 3-5 minutes or until the crust is crispy golden brown and chicken is cooked through. Serve warm with your favorite dip.

Air Fryer Southwest Chicken

Servings: 3
Cooking Time: 19 Minutes

Ingredients:
- 3 boneless chicken breasts 7 ounces each
- 2 tablespoons lime juice
- 1 tablespoon olive oil
- ½ teaspoon chili powder
- ½ teaspoon cumin
- ¼ teaspoon garlic powder
- ¼ teaspoon salt

Directions:
1. Preheat air fryer to 370°F.
2. Toss chicken with seasonings, oil, and lime juice.
3. Place chicken breasts in a single layer in the air fryer basket.
4. Cook for 16-19 minutes flipping chicken after 10 minutes.
5. Rest 5 minutes before slicing.

Notes
Ensure chicken reaches an internal temperature of 165°F. Check the chicken early, do not overcook.
These are great sliced and served in taco shells or tortillas.

Frozen Chicken Cordon Bleu In The Air Fryer

Servings: 2-4
Cooking Time: 20 Minutes

Ingredients:
- 2 to 4 Frozen chicken cordon bleu

Directions:
1. Preheat your air fryer at 380 degrees F.
2. Place chicken cordon bleu in the air fryer
3. Cook for 18-20 minutes. Since these are made with raw chicken it is very important that the internal temperature reaches 165 degrees F. Some cheese may begin to come out, but that is okay.
4. Allow to sit for a few minutes and then serve!

NOTES
HOW TO REHEAT CHICKEN CORDON BLEU IN THE AIR FRYER:
Preheat the air fryer to 350 degrees F.
Place your leftover chicken cordon bleu in the air fryer basket.
Cook for 4 to 5 minutes until warmed through.

Air Fryer Bbq Chicken Thighs

Servings: 4
Cooking Time: 25 Minutes

Ingredients:
- 4 bone-in chicken thighs
- 1 tablespoon olive oil
- 1 teaspoon smoked paprika
- 1 teaspoon garlic powder
- ½ teaspoon onion powder
- ½ teaspoon salt
- ¼ teaspoon black pepper
- ⅛ teaspoon cayenne pepper (optional)
- ½ cup BBQ sauce, homemade or bottled, plus more for serving

Directions:
1. Preheat your air fryer to 400 degrees F for 5 minutes. Pat the chicken thighs dry with paper towels and rub them with olive oil.
2. In a small bowl, combine the paprika, garlic powder, onion powder, salt, pepper, and cayenne. Rub seasoning evenly over chicken thighs.
3. Place the chicken, skin side down, inside; air fry for 12 minutes.
4. Flip the thighs and brush them with half of the BBQ sauce. Air fry for 5 minutes, brush them with the remaining BBQ sauce, then continue cooking for 3-8 more minutes, until cooked to an internal temperature of 165 degrees F. Serve with more BBQ sauce and your desired side dishes.

NOTES
HOW TO REHEAT BBQ CHICKEN THIGHS:
Preheat your air fryer to 400 degrees.
Place chicken in air fryer basket and cook for 5 minutes or until hot all the way through.

Homemade Air Fryer Chicken Nuggets

Servings: 4
Cooking Time: 12 Minutes

Ingredients:
- 1 pound ground chicken
- 1 teaspoon garlic powder
- ½ teaspoon onion powder
- ¼ teaspoon salt
- ¼ teaspoon pepper
- 1 egg
- Breading
- ¾ cup seasoned bread crumbs
- 3 tablespoons panko bread crumbs
- 1 teaspoon oil

Directions:
1. Preheat the air fryer to 375°F.
2. Combine chicken and seasonings in a small bowl.
3. Whisk the egg in a small bowl. Mix the breading mixture in a separate bowl.
4. Create small flat 1 inch discs of the chicken mixture. Dip in the egg and finally into the breading.
5. Spray with cooking oil and place in a single layer in the air fryer basket.
6. Cook for 12-14 minutes flipping the nuggets halfway through cooking.
7. Notes
8. Leftover chicken nuggets will keep in the freezer in an airtight container for up to 4 weeks.

Air Fryer Chicken Thighs With Salsa Verde And Lemony Kale Salad

Servings: 4

Ingredients:
- Deselect All
- Lemony Kale Salad:
- 3 tablespoons lemon juice
- 2 teaspoons Dijon mustard
- 1 teaspoon finely grated zest
- Pinch crushed red pepper flakes
- Kosher salt and freshly ground black pepper
- 5 tablespoons olive oil
- 1 bunch curly kale (about 10 ounces), woody stems removed and leaves very thinly sliced
- 1/2 cup panko
- 1 tablespoon finely grated Pecorino Romano, plus more for serving
- Chicken Thighs:
- Four bone-in skin-on chicken thighs (about 2 pounds total)
- 2 teaspoons finely grated lemon zest
- Kosher salt and freshly ground black pepper
- 1 tablespoon olive oil

- Salsa Verde:
- 2 teaspoons capers
- 2 oil-packed anchovy filets (optional)
- 1 clove garlic
- Kosher salt
- 1/4 cup plus 2 tablespoons olive oil
- 1 teaspoon red wine vinegar
- 1 teaspoon finely grated lemon zest
- 1 cup fresh parsley leaves, finely chopped
- 1 cup fresh basil leaves, finely chopped
- 1/2 small bunch chives, finely chopped (about 1/4 cup chopped)

Directions:
1. Special equipment: a 3.5-quart air fryer and a 6- to 7-inch round baking dish
2. For the lemony kale salad: Whisk the lemon juice, Dijon, lemon zest, pepper flakes, 1 teaspoon salt and several grinds of pepper in a large bowl until combined. Slowly whisk in 3 tablespoons of the olive oil until smooth and emulsified. Add the kale and toss until well coated. Taste and adjust the seasoning with salt and pepper, if needed. Set aside at room temperature to marinate and soften, at least 15 minutes at and up to 8 hours in the refrigerator.
3. Meanwhile, preheat the air fryer to 350 degrees F. Toss together the panko, remaining 2 tablespoons olive oil, a pinch of salt and a few grinds of pepper in a 6- to 7-inch baking dish until evenly combined. Place the baking dish in the air fryer basket and air fry until the panko are golden brown, stirring halfway through, 4 to 6 minutes. Remove the dish from the air fryer, stir in the Pecorino and set aside.
4. For the chicken thighs: Preheat the air fryer to 400 degrees F. Pat the chicken dry between a few paper towels (this will help the skin get crispy). Rub the lemon zest onto the skinless side of each thigh and season with a good pinch of salt and several grinds of pepper. Flip the thighs over, rub the olive oil onto the skin and season each thigh with a good pinch of salt and several grinds of pepper. Place the thighs in the air fryer basket skin-side up, leaving a little space between each piece. Air fry until the skin is crispy and the chicken is browned all over and cooked through, 22 to 25 minutes.
5. For the salsa verde: Meanwhile, finely chop the capers, anchovy filets (if using), garlic and a small pinch of salt with a sharp chef's knife, mashing and scraping the mixture until it becomes a paste. Transfer to a small bowl and stir in the olive oil, vinegar and lemon zest. Fold in the parsley, basil and chives until thoroughly combined. Taste and adjust the seasoning with salt and pepper, if needed.
6. To serve, give the kale salad a good toss, then top with the toasted panko and some more grated Pecorino. Transfer the chicken thighs to a dinner plate or serving platter and spoon the salsa verde over the top. Serve with the kale salad.

Cook's Note

You can make the salsa verde in a food processor by pulsing together all the ingredients until the herbs are finely chopped and the sauce is just combined. (There's no need to chop the herbs first.)

Air Fryer Turkey Legs

Servings: 2
Cooking Time: 25 Minutes

Ingredients:
- 2 turkey legs
- 2 tablespoons unsalted butter melted
- 1/2 teaspoon paprika
- 1/2 teaspoon kosher salt
- 1/2 teaspoon fresh thyme or ground
- 1/2 teaspoon fresh rosemary or ground
- 1/2 teaspoon fresh sage or ground
- 1/4 teaspoon ground black pepper

Directions:
1. In a small mixing bowl, combine the seasonings with the melted butter.
2. Pat the turkey drumsticks dry with a paper towel, then brush the butter and completely coat the turkey legs on both sides.
3. Place the turkey legs in a single layer, in the air fryer basket, then air fry at 400 degrees F for 25-30 minutes cook time, turning halfway through air frying.

4. Confirm doneness using an instant read meat thermometer, the internal temperature should reach 165 degrees.
5. Let the turkey rest for about 5-7 minutes before eating. Serve this amazing dish with your favorite.

Air Fryer Buffalo Wings

Servings: 4
Cooking Time: 22 Minutes

Ingredients:
- 1 pound chicken wings
- 1 tablespoon olive oil
- salt and pepper to taste
- ¾ cup buffalo sauce
- Homemade Buffalo Sauce
- ½ cup franks hot sauce
- ¼ cup butter melted
- pinch garlic powder

Directions:

1. Preheat air fryer to 400°F.
2. Dry wings with a paper towel and toss with oil and seasonings.
3. Place in a single layer in the air fryer basket and cook for 20 minutes, flipping the wings after 10 minutes.
4. Once done remove from the air fryer and toss with buffalo sauce in a bowl.
5. Return to the air fryer and cook for another 2 minutes.

Notes

To feed a crowd: Don't overcrowd the air fryer. To feed a crowd, make batches of wings. Place all batches in the air fryer at 400°F for 2-3 minutes to heat through before serving

For Crispy Chicken Wings: Ensure the wings are really dry before adding the oil, seasonings, and sauce, otherwise they won't adhere.

For a really sticky, thick buffalo sauce, mix in a pinch or two of corn starch before tossing the wings in it.

VEGETABLE & & VEGETARIAN RECIPES

Air Fryer Brussels Sprouts
Servings: 4
Cooking Time: 12 Minutes

Ingredients:
FOR THE BRUSSELS SPROUTS:
- 1 pound Brussels sprouts
- 2 teaspoons extra virgin olive oil
- 1/4 teaspoon kosher salt
- 1/4 teaspoon black pepper
- 3 cloves garlic thinly sliced (optional but delish!)

OPTIONAL TOPPINGS:
- 1 tablespoon balsamic glaze or reduced balsamic vinegar
- Drizzle pomegranate molasses
- 2 teaspoons pure maple syrup
- 3 tablespoons freshly grated Parmesan cheese

Directions:
1. Trim off the ends of the Brussel sprouts and remove any brown outer leaves. Cut them in half from stem to end. If any are very large, cut them into quarters from stem to end so that all the pieces are fairly similar in size and cook evenly.
2. OPTIONAL—This step makes sure the Brussels sprouts a little more tender in the middle; that said, if you don't mind a firmer sprout, you can skip it—I like my Brussels sprouts firm/tender inside and crispy outside, so I typically skip it—Place the Brussels sprouts in a large bowl and cover with warm tap water. Let sit 10 minutes.
3. Preheat the air fryer to 375 degrees, according to the manufacturer's instructions (for my air fryer, that's 3 minutes of preheating).
4. Drain the Brussels sprouts and with a towel, lightly pat dry. Wipe out the bowl you used for soaking, then add the Brussels sprouts back to it (if you didn't soak the sprouts, simply place them in a large mixing bowl). Drizzle with the oil and sprinkle with the salt and black pepper. Toss to coat evenly, then add them to your fryer basket.
5. Cook the sprouts for 5 minutes, then slide out the basket and shake it to toss the Brussels sprouts to promote even cooking. Cook 5 additional minutes, then slide out the basket again. The Brussels sprouts should look like they are getting nice and crispy and are almost done (if not, let them cook a minute or so longer). Add the garlic cloves and toss to coat once more. Cook 2 to 4 additional minutes, checking and shaking the basket often, until the Brussels sprouts are deeply crisp.
6. If adding toppings, transfer the Brussels sprouts to a serving bowl (or wipe out the mixing bowl you previously used) and stir in any desired toppings. Enjoy hot.

Notes
TO STORE: Refrigerate Brussels sprouts in an airtight storage container for up to 4 days.
TO REHEAT: Rewarm leftovers on a baking sheet in the oven at 350 degrees F.
TO FREEZE: The Brussels sprouts will get mushy once thawed, so I don't recommend freezing them. If you have lots leftover, you can freeze them in an airtight freezer-safe storage container for up to 3 months. Let thaw overnight in the refrigerator before reheating.

Hot Cauliflower Wings
Servings: 4

Ingredients:
- For the wings
- 1/2 head of cauliflower, cut into florets
- 1 cup of flour, you can use gluten free flour
- 1 1/2 cup of coconut milk
- 1/2 tsp smoked paprika powder
- 1/3 tsp harrisa powder
- salt and black pepper
- 1/2 tsp garlic powder
- For the sauce
- 1 cup of bbq sauce
- 2 tbsp sweet and sour sauce
- 2 tbsp tomato puree
- 2 tbsp lemon juice
- 2 tbsp honey

- 1 tbsp sriracha sauce (optional)

Directions:
1. Start by chopping cauliflower to smaller florets.
2. Prepare the batter by placing in the bowl; coconut milk, spices, salt & pepper and flour. Mix until everything is well incorporated.
3. Preheat your ninja electric grill on air frying mode to 200C.
4. Coat each cauliflower floret in the batter. Shake off the excess of the batter.
5. Place them in the air fryer cooking basket, don't place them to close together, as they will stick.
6. Once that's done, set the time to 10 min. Shake the florets half way the time, make sure they crisp evenly on both sides.
7. Make the sauce by placing all ingredients in the small pot. Cook for 5-7 min on a medium heat steering. The sauce should thicken a bit.
8. Coat each baked cauliflower florets in the sauce.
9. Serve hot.

Air Fryer Baked Potato

Servings: 1
Cooking Time: 30 Minutes-1 Hour

Ingredients:
- 1 baking potato (see recipe tips and weigh before cooking), scrubbed and dried
- light rapeseed, vegetable or sunflower oil
- salt and freshly ground black pepper
- For the cheddar and jalapeño topping
- small handful grated cheddar
- 1 ripe tomato, diced
- few green jalapeño pepper slices from a jar
- For the smashed avocado topping
- 1 small, ripe avocado (or a few frozen avocado slices)
- ½ lime or lemon, juice only
- handful mixed seeds, dukkah, za'atar or chilli flakes
- For the curried beans topping
- 227g tin baked beans
- ½ tsp curry powder
- natural yoghurt and lime pickle (optional), to serve

Directions:
1. Rub the potato all over with a little oil. If you like, rub a little salt over the skin – this will help give a crispier finish.
2. Put the potato in the air fryer and turn to 200C (you don't want to preheat, to avoid burning the skin before the inside is cooked.) Air-fry for 20 minutes, then turn the potato over. A small potato will take another 20 minutes or so, a large one another 25–30 minutes.
3. Check the middle is soft by poking a table knife into the centre – it should slide in easily. If it's not quite done, continue to cook for a minute at a time.
4. For the cheddar and jalapeño topping, mix the cheese, tomato and jalapeño slices, split the potato and spoon the cheese mixture on top.
5. For the smashed avocado topping, mash the avocado with the lime or lemon juice, salt and pepper. Split the potato, spoon in the avocado mixture and scatter with the seeds or your choice of seasoning.
6. For the curried beans topping, heat the beans with the curry powder until hot but not boiling. Split the potato and pile on the beans. Top with dollops of yoghurt and lime pickle, if using.

NOTES

Small potatoes, around 225g/8oz each, will be ready in 40 minutes. Large potatoes, around 350g/12oz each, will take 45–50 minutes to get soft inside.

You can speed up the cooking by microwaving your jacket potatoes first. Microwave on high power for four minutes, turn the potato over, and microwave for another four minutes. (If you are cooking two potatoes, you may need to microwave them for an extra 2 minutes.) Then cook in the air-fryer for 10 minutes to crisp up.

Look for potatoes labelled as bakers, or a floury variety, such as King Edward, Maris Piper, Vivaldi or Estima.

Smashed Potatoes
Servings: 3
Cooking Time: 35 Minutes
Ingredients:
- 2 lbs small (900 g) potatoes
- 1/2 tbsp salt for boiling + more for sprinkling
- 1 1/2 tbsp oil for brushing
- Fresh parsley to garnish
- Onion powder, garlic powder, black pepper to sprinkle (optional)

Directions:
1. You can watch the short video for visual instructions.
2. Heat water in a large pot, stir in the salt, and add the potatoes (they should be covered with water by 1 inch / 5 cm). Cook the potatoes for about 20 minutes or until fork-tender, then drain the water. The time depends on the size of the potatoes.
3. If you plan on making the smashed potatoes in your oven, then also preheat your oven to 400 °F (205 °C).
4. Transfer the cooked potatoes to a large greased baking sheet and smash each potato using a glass.
5. Brush the smashed potatoes with the oil, sprinkle them with salt and bake for about 35-45 minutes or until golden (they might be done earlier, depending on your oven). Broil at the end for some minutes, for extra crispiness.
6. I prefer cooking them in my air fryer for 15-18 minutes at 380 °F (190 °C).
7. Sprinkle with black pepper, onion powder, and garlic powder (optional). Garnish with fresh parsley and enjoy with this avocado pesto!

Notes
Salt the water liberally: Potatoes require a lot of salt to absorb a good amount of flavor, so don't be shy.
Don't skimp on oil: This will cling to all the fluffy smashed edges and help your roasted smashed potatoes become super crispy.
For the crispiest results: It can help to let the potatoes steam dry for some minutes before cooking them, as the lower moisture levels yields crispier skins.
Messy smashed potatoes are fine: All the extra ridges and fluffy bits will make it even crispier. I specifically recommend NOT smashing them too neatly!

Ginger And Soy Salmon Fillets With Broccoli
Servings: 2
Ingredients:
- Deselect All
- 2 cups small broccoli florets
- 2 tablespoons vegetable oil
- Kosher salt and freshly ground black pepper
- 1 tablespoon soy sauce
- 1 teaspoon light brown sugar
- 1 teaspoon rice vinegar
- 1/4 teaspoon cornstarch
- One 1/2-inch piece ginger, peeled and grated
- 2 skin-on salmon fillets (6 ounces each)
- 1 scallion, thinly sliced
- Cooked white rice, for serving

Directions:
1. Toss the broccoli with 1 tablespoon of the oil in a bowl until coated. Season with salt and pepper. Transfer the broccoli to a 3.5-quart air fryer.
2. Stir together the soy sauce, sugar, vinegar, cornstarch and ginger in a small bowl. Brush the salmon fillets on all sides with the remaining 1 tablespoon oil, then with the sauce. Arrange the salmon flesh-side down on top of the broccoli.
3. Cook at 375 degrees F until the broccoli is tender and the salmon is cooked through, 10 to 12 minutes for medium to well done, depending on the thickness of your fillets. Transfer to serving plates, sprinkle with the scallion slices and serve with rice.

NOTES
You can substitute 2 tablespoons store-bought teriyaki sauce for the soy sauce, brown sugar and vinegar. If light brown sugar isn't available, feel free to use dark brown sugar.

Air Fryer Potato Gratin
Servings: 6
Cooking Time: 45 Minutes
Ingredients:
- 750 grams potatoes, peeled
- 2/3 cup (160ml) pouring cream, warmed
- 1/3 cup (80ml) milk, warmed
- 1 tablespoon rosemary leaves
- 2 cloves garlic, crushed
- 1 small onion (80g), sliced thinly
- 1 cup (120g) grated gruyère cheese
- to serve: sea salt flakes

Directions:
1. Using a mandoline, V-slicer or sharp knife, slice potatoes very thinly.
2. Whisk cream, milk, rosemary and garlic in a large jug until combined, then season.
3. Layer potato slices, onion and cream mixture in a 20cm (8in) round ovenproof dish, finishing with the cream mixture. Using your hands, press down on the potatoes firmly.
4. Preheat a 7-litre air fryer to 160°C/325°F for 3 minutes.
5. Taking care, place the dish in the air fryer basket; at 160°C/325°F, cook for 25 minutes until potatoes are just tender.
6. Scatter potatoes with gruyère; at 160°C/325°F, cook for a further 5 minutes or until cheese is golden.
7. Sprinkle gratin with salt flakes to serve.

Air Fryer Fried Green Tomatoes
Servings: 4
Cooking Time: 10 Minutes
Ingredients:
- 4 large green tomatoes firm
- 2 large eggs
- 1/4 cup milk
- 1 cup flour
- 1/2 teaspoon salt
- 1/4 teaspoon pepper
- 1/2 cup cornmeal
- 1/2 cup breadcrumbs
- 2 Tablespoon grated parmesan
- 1 tablespoon Italian seasoning
- olive oil spray

Directions:
1. In a small bowl add the eggs and whisk. Add in the milk. In another small bowl add the flour, salt, and pepper. In another small bowl add the cornmeal, bread crumbs, and parmesan cheese.
2. Dredge each tomato slice first in the eggs, then coat in the flour, and lastly the cornmeal mix. Add the tomatoes to the basket of an air fryer and spray the tops with olive oil spray.
3. Cook at 400 degrees in the air fryer for 5-6 minutes, then flip over and spray with olive oil and cook for an additional 5 minutes.

Keto Fried Pickles
Servings: 4
Cooking Time: 7 Minutes
Ingredients:
- 9 large pickles sliced lengthways
- 3/4 + 1 tablespoon almond flour
- 1/2 teaspoon salt
- 1/4 teaspoon pepper
- 1 cup parmesan cheese
- 2 large eggs
- 2 tablespoons sour cream

Directions:
1. Slice your dill pickles lengthways and set aside.
2. In a small bowl, add your almond flour, salt, pepper, and parmesan cheese and mix until combined. In a separate bowl, whisk together the eggs and sour cream.
3. Dip the dill pickles in the wet mixture, followed by the dry mixture. Repeat the process until all the pickles are battered.
4. Add some oil to a non-stick pan. Once hot, add the battered pickles to it and fry for 3-4 minutes, flipping halfway through, until golden brown.
5. Serve the fried pickles immediately with your favorite condiments.

Notes
If you'd like to make this in an air fryer, simply prepare as instructed. Once ready to cook, add

them to an air fryer basket and air fry at 200C/400F for 8 minutes.
TO STORE: Leftover pickles should be stored in the refrigerator, covered, for up to three days.
TO FREEZE: Place the cooked and cooled pickles in an airtight container and store them in the freezer for up to two months.
REHEAT: As the fried pickles are 'battered', they should not be microwaved. Instead, reheat them in the air fryer or in a preheated oven.

Air Fryer Broccoli And Cauliflower

Servings: 4
Cooking Time: 8 Minutes

Ingredients:
- 2 cups broccoli florets cut into bite size pieces
- 2 cups cauliflower florets cut into bite size pieces
- 2 tablespoons extra virgin olive oil
- 1 teaspoon garlic powder
- 1/2 teaspoon kosher salt

Directions:
1. In a large bowl, add fresh broccoli and fresh cauliflower.
2. Then add in olive oil, garlic powder, and salt, tossing together until vegetables are well coated.
3. Spray olive oil spray into the basket to make sure vegetables get crispier edges and do not stick.
4. Pour vegetables into the air fryer basket. Air fry at 380 degrees F for 8-10 minutes until the vegetables have crisp edges and are golden brown.
5. Toss or shake the basket halfway through the cooking process.
6. Serve while hot.

NOTES
Optional Additional Toppings: Fresh lemon juice and zest, sautéed bell peppers, sprinkle of parmesan cheese, lemon zest or creamy cheese sauce.
Cooking Tips: You can cut and season the florets in advance which makes meal prep even easier. Precut florets can be found in the produce section of your local grocery store, just be sure and cut larger pieces so every piece is bite size.

Substitutions: Use refined coconut oil, avocado oil or vegetable oil in place of olive oil.

Air Fryer Squash Soup

Servings: 4

Ingredients:
- 2 1/2 lb. butternut squash, peeled, cut into 1-inch pieces
- 2 medium carrots, cut into 1-inch pieces
- 1 large onion, cut into 1/2-inch-thick wedges
- 4 cloves garlic, 2 whole and 2 thinly sliced, divided
- 1 Fresno chile, seeded
- 4 sprigs fresh thyme
- 4 tbsp. olive oil, divided
- Kosher salt
- 2 tbsp. pepitas
- 1/4 tsp. smoked paprika
- Sour cream and crusty bread, for serving

Directions:
1. In large bowl, toss squash, carrots, onion, whole garlic cloves, chile, thyme, 2 tablespoons oil and 3/4 teaspoon salt. Transfer to air-fryer basket and air-fry at 400°F, shaking basket occasionally, until vegetables are tender, 30 minutes. Discard thyme sprigs.
2. Meanwhile, in small skillet on medium, cook sliced garlic in remaining 2 tablespoons oil, stirring, until garlic begins to lightly brown around the edges, 2 minutes. Add pepitas and paprika and a pinch of salt and cook 1 minute; transfer to a bowl.
3. Transfer all but 1/2 cup squash to blender, add 1 cup water and puree, gradually adding 3 more cups water, pureeing until smooth. Reheat if necessary and serve topped with sour cream and spiced pepitas and with crusty bread if desired. Serve topped with remaining squash.
4. GH Test Kitchen Tip: Freeze leftover soup (without the cream and seeds) in an airtight container for up to 3 months. Thaw overnight in the refrigerator, then warm and top as desired.

Air Fryer Herbed Brussels Sprouts

Servings: 4
Cooking Time: 8 Minutes

Ingredients:
- 1 lb. brussels sprouts (cleaned and trimmed)
- ½ tsp. dried thyme
- 1 tsp. dried parsley
- 1 tsp. garlic powder (Or 4 cloves, minced)
- ¼ tsp. salt
- 2 tsp. oil

Directions:
1. Remove any outer leaves of the brussels sprouts that don't look healthy. Lightly cook your brussels sprouts, either by boiling them for 13-15 minutes or by microwaving them on high for about 3-4 minutes.
2. Cut them in half.
3. Place all ingredients in a medium or large mixing bowl and toss to coat the brussels sprouts evenly.
4. Pour them into the food basket of the air fryer and close it up.
5. Set the heat to 390 F. and the time to 8 minutes. This setting roasts them nicely on the outside while leaving the insides a nicely cooked al dente.
6. Cool slightly and serve.

Notes
Please note that the nutrition data below is a ballpark figure. Exact data is not possible.

Air Fryer Cauliflower Recipe

Servings: 4
Cooking Time: 7 Minutes

Ingredients:
- 1 head Cauliflower (cut into florets)
- 3 tbsp Olive oil
- 2 tsp Lemon juice
- 3/4 tsp Smoked paprika
- 1/2 tsp Garlic powder
- 1/2 tsp Sea salt
- 1/4 tsp Black pepper

Directions:
1. Preheat the air fryer to 380 degrees F (193 degrees C).
2. Place the cauliflower florets in a large bowl. Drizzle with olive oil and lemon juice. Season with smoked paprika, garlic powder, sea salt, and black pepper. Toss to coat.
3. Add cauliflower to the air fryer basket in a single layer (cook in batches if needed – don't crowd the basket). Cook cauliflower in the air fryer for 7-10 minutes (depending on the size of your florets), shaking the basket halfway through, until browned on the edges.

Air Fryer Broccoli

Servings: 4
Cooking Time: 14 Minutes

Ingredients:
- 1 head broccoli cut in florets
- 1 tablespoon olive oil
- salt and pepper to taste

Directions:
1. Preheat the air fryer to 390°F.
2. Toss broccoli with the oil and seasonings in a large bowl.
3. Put in the air fryer basket and cook for 12-14 minutes or until broccoli is tender.

Notes
For best results, cut broccoli florets into evenly sized florets and avoid overcrowding.
Keep warm in the oven while cooking in batches and reheat leftovers in the air fryer for a few minutes to crisp back up!

Air Fryer Zucchini

Servings: 4
Cooking Time: 10 Minutes

Ingredients:
- 2 large zucchini sliced into coins
- 1 tablespoon olive oil
- 1/2 teaspoon salt
- 1/2 teaspoon pepper

Directions:
1. In a large mixing bowl, add your sliced zucchini, olive oil, salt, and pepper, and mix well.

2. Transfer the zucchini into an air fryer basket or, if you'd like grill marks, add the grill pan to an air fryer basket. Cook the zucchini for 10 minutes at 200C/400F, shaking the basket every 3 minutes.
3. Remove the zucchini from the air fryer and serve immediately.

Notes
TO STORE: Zucchini can be stored in the refrigerator, covered. It will keep well for up to 5 days.
TO FREEZE: Place leftover zucchini in a shallow container and store it in the freezer for up to 2 months.
TO REHEAT: If the pre-frozen zucchini has been thawed (or previously refrigerated), you can add it to the air fryer basket and reheat at 200C/400F for 4 minutes, flipping halfway through.

Air Fryer Pickles

Servings: 4
Cooking Time: 6 Minutes

Ingredients:
- 36 large pickle slices
- 1 cup Panko bread crumbs
- 1 large egg
- ½ tablespoon water
- ½ cup all-purpose flour
- ½ teaspoon garlic powder
- ½ teaspoon paprika
- ½ teaspoon dried dill

Directions:
1. Drain pickles well and lay them on a few layers of paper towels, drying them well.
2. Preheat the air fryer to 400 degrees F.
3. In a wide, shallow bowl, place Panko crumbs. In a second bowl, whisk egg with water. In a third bowl, whisk together the flour, garlic powder, paprika, and dill.
4. Dredge each pickle through the flour mixture, dip them in the egg, then press them into the Panko to coat.
5. Spray the air fryer basket with cooking spray, then carefully place a single layer of pickles in the basket. Work in batches as necessary. Lightly spray the tops of the pickles with cooking spray, then cook for 4 minutes. Flip the pickles and cook them for an additional 2-4 minutes, until they're browned and crispy.
6. Allow to cool slightly before serving with your favorite dipping sauce.

NOTES
HOW TO REHEAT FRIED PICKLES:
Preheat your air fryer to 350 degrees.
Add fried pickles to the basket.
Cook for 3 minutes or until hot.

Air Fryer Vegetarian Pumpkin Schnitzel

Servings: 2
Cooking Time: 30 Minutes

Ingredients:
- 500g potatoes, peeled, cut into 3-4cm pieces
- 250g swede or turnip, peeled, cut into 3-4cm pieces
- 2 1/2 tbsp extra virgin olive oil
- 1/2 cup Panko breadcrumbs
- 1/4 cup finely grated cheddar
- 2 tbsp finely chopped hazelnuts
- 1 tbsp finely chopped flat-leaf parsley, plus extra to serve
- 500g butternut pumpkin, peeled
- 1 egg
- Lemon wedges, to serve
- Select all Ingredients:

Directions:
1. Place potatoes and turnip in a medium saucepan and cover with water. Season with salt. Bring to the boil over high heat. Gently boil, covered, for 15 minutes or until tender. Drain well and return to pan. Add 2 tablespoons oil and mash until smooth. Season with salt and pepper.
2. Meanwhile, Preheat Philips Airfryer to 180C.
3. Combine breadcrumbs, cheddar, hazelnuts, parsley and remaining oil in a shallow dish. Season with salt and pepper. Cut pumpkin into 1cm thick slices. Lightly beat egg on a shallow plate.
4. Dip pumpkin into egg to cover all over. Press into breadcrumb mixture to coat all over. Place in the basket, using the grill

separator to arrange a second layer of pumpkin. Insert basket into Airfryer. Cook for 12 minutes or until golden and tender.
5. Serve pumpkin schnitzels with mash and lemon wedges. Sprinkle with extra chopped parsley.

Air Fryer Cauliflower
Servings: 4
Cooking Time: 13 Minutes
Ingredients:
- 1 head cauliflower florets
- 1 tablespoon olive oil
- salt and pepper to taste

Directions:
1. Preheat the air fryer to 390°F.
2. Toss the cauliflower with oil and seasonings in a large bowl.
3. Place in the air fryer basket and cook for 12-13 minutes, shaking the basket halfway through cooking.
4. Notes
5. Store leftover cauliflower in an airtight container in the fridge for up to 4-5 days. Reheat in the air fryer or under the broiler until crispy.

Air Fryer Twice-baked Potatoes
Ingredients:
- 1 medium baking potato
- 1 Tbsp olive oil
- Salt & pepper
- 1 Tbsp butter, softened
- ½ Tbsp 2% milk
- 1.5 oz cream cheese
- 1 Tbsp sour cream
- Green onions (optional)

Directions:
1. Pierce potato and brush lightly with olive oil. Sprinkle outside with salt and pepper.
2. Bake in your air fryer for 15 minutes at 400°F. Flip and bake for 15 additional minutes.
3. Set aside potato to cool. When cool enough to handle, cut in half lengthwise, then scoop out pulp, leaving a thin shell.
4. In a small bowl, mash the pulp with butter, milk, and a pinch of salt. Stir in cream cheese and sour cream. Spoon into potato shells.
5. Return potatoes to air fryer. Bake, uncovered, until heated through and the tops are golden brown, approximately 15 minutes. Top with sliced green onions, if desired. Enjoy!

Air Fryer Stuffed Peppers
Servings: 4
Cooking Time: 22 Minutes
Ingredients:
- 4 medium bell peppers
- 1 pound Italian sausage
- ½ onion diced
- ½ cup instant rice
- ½ teaspoon basil
- ½ teaspoon oregano
- ½ cup water
- ¼ cup parmesan cheese
- 2 cups pasta sauce divided
- ½ cup mozzarella cheese shredded

Directions:
1. Preheat air fryer to 320°F.
2. Cut the tops off the bell peppers and remove any seeds. (*see note)
3. Brush with oil and place the peppers in the air fryer for 5-6 minutes.
4. Brown sausage and onions in medium skillet. Drain any fat.
5. Add rice, seasonings, water, and 1 cup pasta sauce to the sausage mixture. Bring to a boil, reduce heat, and simmer 3-4 minutes. Remove from heat and stir in parmesan cheese.
6. Fill the peppers with the sausage mixture. Top with remaining sauce and place in the air fryer basket.
7. Turn the air fryer to 350°F, and cook the peppers for 8-10 minutes. Top with mozzarella and cook for 1-2 minutes, or

until the cheese is melted and slightly browned.

Notes

If your peppers are large, cut them lengthwise so they do not touch the top of the basket.

If your peppers don't sit flat, use aluminum foil to hold them upright.

If your peppers are small you may need a couple more than listed in the recipe.

Cajun Prawns With Potato & Corn

Servings: 4

Ingredients:
- 500g baby new potatoes
- 1 tbsp olive oil
- 4 corn on the cobs
- 300g king prawns, shell on
- 2 tsp Cajun spice
- 1 tbsp fresh lemon juice
- 2 tbsp unsalted butter
- 2 tsp Worcestershire sauce
- Fresh cracked pepper, to taste
- Flaked sea salt, to taste
- Lemon wedges, for serving
- Optional for serving
- 2 sprigs fresh thyme, leaves picked from stems and roughly chopped
- 4 sprigs parsley, chopped

Directions:
1. Insert crisper paniere in pan and place pan in unit. Preheat unit by selecting AIR FRY, set temperature to 180°C and set time to 3 minutes. Select START/STOP to begin.
2. In a bowl, toss potatoes with oil. In a separate bowl, combine corn, prawns, cajun spice, lemon juice, butter, Worcestershire sauce, pepper and salt. Toss to combine and reserve.
3. Once unit has preheated, remove pan and place potatoes on crisper paniere. Reinsert pan, select AIR FRY, set temperature to 180°C and set time for 20 minutes. Select START/STOP to begin.
4. After 15 minutes, remove pan and add corn and prawn mixture. Shake well to combine, then reinsert pan to resume cooking for an additional 5 minutes.
5. After 20 total minutes, remove pan and place food on panierter. Serve with lemon wedges and fresh herbs, if desired.

TIP For even more flavour, pour any leftover butter or juices from cooking over the finished dish.

Crispy Air Fryer Brussels Sprouts

Ingredients:
- 1 lb. brussels sprouts, trimmed and halved lengthwise (approximately 4 cups)
- 1 tablespoon olive oil
- 1/2 tablespoon Italian seasoning
- 1/2 tablespoon garlic powder
- 1/8 teaspoon salt
- 1/4 teaspoon ground black pepper, or to taste

Directions:
1. Combine all ingredients in a large bowl and toss to combine and coat brussels sprouts evenly. Transfer brussels sprouts to air fryer basket.
2. Turn air fryer on to 350 F and cook for 12 minutes, until brussels sprouts are cooked through and golden brown on the edges.

NOTES

These instructions work best with a Philips Air Fryer (1.8 lb/2.75 qt). If you have larger or smaller air fryer, you will have to adjust the cook time. Just check in on the brussels sprouts every 5 minutes to make sure that it cooks through and that they don't burn.

Air Fryer Fried Pickles
Servings: 4
Cooking Time: 10 Minutes

Ingredients:
- 2 cups dill pickle slices
- 1/2 cup flour
- 1 large egg
- 1 Tablespoon water
- 1/2 cup bread crumbs
- 1/4 cup grated Parmesan
- 1 Tablespoon Italian seasoning

Directions:
1. Lay the pickles on a paper towel and pat dry. In the first small bowl add the flour. In the second small bowl add the egg and whisk with the water. In the last bowl add the bread crumbs, parmesan, and italian seasoning.
2. Dip each pickle in the flour, then the egg and lastly in the bread crumb mixture.
3. Lay the pickles in a single layer in the air fryer basket. Cook at 400 degrees for 8-10 minutes. Serve with your favorite dipping sauce.

Air Fryer Vegetables
Servings: 4
Cooking Time: 9 Minutes

Ingredients:
- 1 small zucchini sliced
- 2 bell peppers diced
- 1 ½ tablespoon olive oil
- 1 teaspoon Italian seasoning
- 1 garlic clove minced
- salt and pepper to taste

Directions:
1. Preheat air fryer to 380°F.
2. In a large bowl mix vegetables, garlic, seasonings, and oil together until evenly coated.
3. Add to the air fryer basket and cook for 7-9 minutes or until tender-crisp.

Notes
Cut veggies in uniformly and avoid overfilling the air fryer so the veggies evenly cook.

Air Fryer Corn On The Cob
Servings: 4
Cooking Time: 10 Minutes

Ingredients:
- 4 ears corn on the cob
- 1 tablespoon olive oil
- 4 tablespoons butter for serving, optional
- salt & pepper optional

Directions:
1. Preheat the air fryer to 400°F.
2. Brush the corn with olive oil and cook 10-12 minutes, turning occasionally.
3. While corn is cooking, melt butter. Brush butter over the corn and season with salt & pepper to taste.

Notes
Preheat the air fryer before adding the corn.
Peel the corn and rinse any silk and dab them dry before brushing with oil.
Corn can be cooked in batches and kept warm using the warm setting or setting the air fryer to 170°F.
The easiest way to butter corn is to melt the butter and brush it with butter.

SALADS & SIDE DISHES RECIPES

Cardamom Roasted Beetroot Salad With Harissa Tahini Sauce
Servings: 4

Ingredients:
- For the roasted beets
- 500g beetroot (peeled, chopped into 2cm pieces)
- 1 x 400g organic chickpeas (drained, rinsed, patted dry)
- 1 1/2 tbsp olive oil
- 1 tbsp agave nectar
- 2 tsp ground cumin
- 16 Seeds from green cardamom pods (ground in pestle and mortar)
- 1 1/4 tsp sea salt
- 1/2 tsp garlic powder
- 1/4 tsp ground black pepper
- 1 Zest of lemon
- For the sauce
- 80g light tahini
- 190ml lukewarm water
- 1 tbsp rose harissa
- 2 tsp agave nectar
- 1 clove garlic (peeled)
- 1 tsp red wine vinegar
- 1/4 tsp ground cumin
- 1/4 - 1/2 tsp sea salt
- 1/2 - 1 Juice of whole lemon
- For the salad
- 100g pomegranate seeds (roughly 1/2 pomegranate)
- 60g rocket
- 30g walnuts (roughly chopped)
- 20g fresh parsley (roughly chopped)
- 1/2 tsp za'atar
- COOKING MODE
- When entering cooking mode - We will enable your screen to stay 'always on' to avoid any unnecessary interruptions whilst you cook!

Directions:
1. Toss together all of the ingredients for the roasted beets in a large bowl until everything is fully coated.
2. Place the crisper tray into the zone 1 drawer then add the vegetables and insert the drawer back into the unit. Select ROAST, set the temperature to 180°C and the temperature to 25 minutes. Select START/STOP to begin cooking. Shake the drawer every 10 minutes until the cooking time is complete. Remove the drawer and set to one side.
3. Place the ingredients for the sauce into a bullet style blender and blend until smooth. Start with the juice of half a lemon and add more if you feel it needs it. Again if you'd prefer a thinner sauce blend in more water.
4. Toss together the roasted beetroot mixture in a large salad bowl with the remaining salad ingredients then serve immediately with plenty of the sauce drizzled over.

Air Fryer Roasted Butternut Squash Salad
Servings: 4
Cooking Time: 15 Minutes

Ingredients:
- 1 small butternut squash, peeled, seeded, cut into 1-inch pieces
- 4 tablespoons olive oil
- 1 teaspoon 's House Seasoning
- 1/4 teaspoon cayenne pepper
- 2 tablespoons fresh lemon juice
- 1 small shallot, minced
- 1/4 teaspoon salt
- 6 ounces arugula
- 1 small Granny Smith apple, cored and thinly sliced
- 1/2 cup toasted sliced almonds
- 1/2 cup grated Parmesan cheese

Directions:
1. In a large bowl, combine squash, 2 tablespoons of the olive oil, House Seasoning, and cayenne pepper; toss to coat well.
2. Place squash in air fryer basket, set air fryer temperature to 400 degrees, and cook for 15 minutes, shaking occasionally. Let cool.
3. In a large bowl, whisk together lemon juice, shallot, salt, and remaining olive oil. Add

arugula and toss to coat. Divide arugula between 4 salad plates and top with squash and apple slices. Sprinkle with sliced almonds and Parmesan cheese. Serve chilled.

Air Fryer Pigs In A Blanket
Servings: 10
Cooking Time: 8 Minutes

Ingredients:
- 1 can crescent rolls
- 24 cocktail sausages

Directions:
1. Preheat the air fryer to 350 degrees Fahrenheit. Prepare the air fryer basket with nonstick cooking spray, or once the air fryer has been preheated, add parchment paper.
2. Take a pizza cutter and slice each crescent dough sheet into thirds.
3. Take the cut crescent dough and wrap the dough around the sausage.
4. Place the crescent dogs into the prepared air fryer basket in a single layer and make sure to allow an inch or two between each crescent sausage. You may need to cook in batches if needed.
5. Air fry on 350 degrees Fahrenheit for 3-4 minutes, flip, and then air fry for an additional 3-4 minutes, or until the crescents are golden brown.
6. Carefully remove from the air fryer basket and serve with your favorite dipping sauces.

NOTES
This recipe was made using the Cosori 5.8 qt air fryer. If you are using a different air fryer, your cook time may need to be adjusted up or down depending on the wattage and power of the heating element.
WHAT DIPPING SAUCES CAN I USE FOR PIGS IN A BLANKET?
I love to use ketchup and mustard, but you can also use bbq sauce, cheese sauce, honey mustard sauce, ranch dressing, and more.
CAN I COOK FROZEN PIGS IN A BLANKET IN THE AIR FRYER?
Absolutely! If you are cooking these pigs in a blanket from frozen, you will want to add a minute or two to the cooking time to ensure they are cooked completely.

Air Fryer Asparagus Salad With Feta Vinaigrette
Servings: 4

Ingredients:
- 1 lb. asparagus
- 2 tbsp. olive oil, divided
- Kosher salt and pepper
- 1 tbsp. rice vinegar
- 1 small shallot, finely chopped
- 1/4 c. fresh mint, finely chopped
- 2 oz. feta, crumbled
- 2 tbsp. fresh dill, roughly chopped

Directions:
1. Heat oven to 425°F. On a small rimmed baking sheet, toss asparagus with 1 tablespoon oil and ¼ teaspoon each salt and pepper. Roast until just tender, 8 to 12 minutes; transfer to platter.
2. Meanwhile, in small bowl, combine vinegar, shallot and ¼ teaspoon each salt and pepper. Let sit, tossing occasionally, until asparagus is done.
3. Stir remaining tablespoon oil into shallot mixture, then gently toss with mint and feta. Spoon over asparagus and sprinkle with dill.
4. AIR FRYING INSTRUCTIONS:
5. Heat air fryer to 400°F. Toss asparagus with 1 tablespoon olive oil and 1/4 teaspoon each salt and pepper. Air-fry, shaking basket halfway through, until tender, 10 minutes. Proceed with steps 2-3.

Crispy Parmesan Potato Wedges
Servings: 2

Ingredients:
- 2 small russet potatoes
- 2 tablespoons (28 grams) Parmesan cheese, grated
- ¾ teaspoon (4 grams) salt
- ¼ teaspoon (2 grams) garlic powder

- ¼ teaspoon (2 grams) paprika
- ¼ teaspoon (2 grams) dried oregano
- 1 tablespoon (15 milliliters) neutral-flavored oil

Directions:
1. Cut each potato lengthwise into 8 wedges and place them in a large bowl.
2. Add the remaining ingredients and toss to coat.
3. Place the crisper plate into the Smart Air Fryer basket, then place the potatoes onto the crisper plate.
4. Select the Fries function, adjust time to 22 minutes, and press Start/Pause.
5. Remove the potato wedges when done and serve.

Air Fryer Roasted Garlic
Servings: 1/2
Cooking Time: 10 Minutes

Ingredients:
- 3 full bulbs garlic
- 1-2 tablespoons olive oil
- 1 teaspoon salt

Directions:
1. Preheat air fryer to 400 F
2. Carefully slice the tops off the garlic bulbs; the cloves inside should be exposed.
3. Drizzle the olive oil over top of each garlic bulb, making sure all the cloves get covered.
4. Sprinkle salt on each bulb and tightly wrap each in tin foil.
5. Place garlic into your air fryer and cook for 18-20 minutes, or until garlic is tender.
6. Allow to cool until you can handle and remove the bulbs from the papery skin.

Air Fryer Garlic Knots
Servings: 6
Cooking Time: 8 Minutes

Ingredients:
- 1 can store-bought pizza dough 13.8 ounces or two cans of thin crust pizza 8 ounces each
- 4 tablespoons unsalted butter melted
- 1/4 cup parmesan cheese grated
- 2 cloves garlic minced
- 1 tablespoon dried parsley flakes
- 1 teaspoon Italian Seasoning

Directions:
1. Open the can of premade pizza dough and on a lightly floured surface, roll it out into a rectangle.
2. With a pizza cutter or kitchen knife cut the dough into twelve 1-inch strips, and then fold each strip in half. Tie each piece into dough knots, making 12 knots.
3. Place the dough balls into the air fryer basket in a single layer, lined with parchment paper, a silicone baking mat or lightly sprayed with olive oil spray.
4. Air fry at 350 degrees F for 8-10 minutes, until they are golden brown.
5. While knots are in a small mixing bowl, stir together the melted butter, parmesan cheese, garlic, parsley flakes, and Italian seasoning.
6. When knots are golden brown, use a pastry brush and generously brush garlic butter on each piece with butter and seasonings and top with grated parmesan cheese.

NOTES
Kitchen Tips: Make these in batches without overcrowding the basket. Use a food scale to ensure they are all the same size, so they cook evenly. To get a deeper brown color cook for 1 additional minute.
If using regular crust dough, knots will be just a tad bit thicker and may need 1-2 additional minutes of air frying time.
For smaller bites, just cut the dough in half, and you will have 24 garlic knots.
Optional Favorite Dipping Sauce: Our favorite sauce for dipping is marinara. But you can use other sauces, like homemade marinara sauce, alfredo sauce, pesto sauce, pizza sauce or Greek yogurt with roasted garlic.

Artichoke Wings With Vegan Ranch Dip

Servings: 6

Ingredients:
- Artichoke Wings
- One 16-ounce jar marinated artichoke hearts
- 1½ cups all-purpose flour
- 1 teaspoon garlic powder
- 1 teaspoon onion powder
- 1 teaspoon paprika
- 1 teaspoon kosher salt
- One 12-ounce bottle beer (Lager or Weisse-style for best results)
- 2 cups panko breadcrumbs
- Vegan Ranch Dip
- 1 cup vegan mayonnaise
- ¼ cup non-dairy milk (i.e., coconut, oat, or any nut milk)
- 2 tablespoons fresh dill, finely chopped
- 1 teaspoon fresh Italian parsley leaves, finely chopped
- 1 teaspoon vegan Worcestershire sauce (optional)
- 1 teaspoon apple cider vinegar
- 1 teaspoon lemon juice
- 1 clove garlic, grated
- 1 teaspoon onion powder
- 1 teaspoon black pepper
- Kosher salt, to taste
- Oil spray

Directions:
1. Select the Preheat function on the Air Fryer then press Start/Pause.
2. Drain the artichoke hearts and pat dry with paper towels.
3. Whisk together the flour, garlic powder, onion powder, paprika, and salt in a large bowl until evenly distributed.
4. Pour in the beer and whisk well until no lumps remain. The mixture should resemble pancake batter.
5. Place the panko breadcrumbs in a separate medium bowl.
6. Line the preheated air fryer baskets with parchment paper.
7. Dredge the artichoke hearts in the beer batter, then roll in the panko breadcrumbs.
8. Shake off any excess breadcrumbs, then place the dredged artichoke hearts into the lined air fryer baskets.
9. Spray the wings lightly with oil and insert into the preheated air fryer.
10. Adjust temperature to 400°F and time to 10 minutes, press Shake, then press Start/Pause.
11. Flip the wings and spray again halfway through cooking. The Shake Reminder will let you know when.
12. Combine all the dressing ingredients in a separate medium bowl and whisk together.
13. Season to taste with kosher salt. Pour into a bowl for dipping.
14. Remove the artichoke wings from the air fryer when done.
15. Serve immediately with the vegan ranch dressing.

Air Fryer Sweet Potato Casserole

Servings: 6
Cooking Time: 10 Minutes

Ingredients:
- 29 ounce sweet potato yams drained
- 3/4 cup pecans
- 1/4 teaspoon salt
- 1 egg
- 1/2 teaspoon vanilla extract
- 1/4 teaspoon ground cinnamon
- 1 1/4 cup granulated white sugar
- 1 Tablespoon heavy cream
- 2 Tablespoons unsalted butter softened

Directions:
1. Preheat the air fryer to 350 degrees Fahrenheit.
2. Place the sweet potatoes into a medium sized mixing bowl. Add the salt, butter, egg, vanilla extract, ground cinnamon, white sugar, and heavy cream. Mix thoroughly for one minute.
3. Place the pecans in a food processor. Chop the pecans until they are small and easy to sprinkle.
4. Take the sweet potato mixture and place in a prepared 7" springform pan. Cover the top with the chopped pecans.

5. Place the springform pan into the air fryer basket. Air fry for 10-12 minutes or until the topping is browned.

NOTES

Can I make a sweet potato casserole in the air fryer with a marshmallow topping?

Yes, you can, but you may want to consider doing it a little differently than the traditional method of topping the casserole with mini marshmallows. Because marshmallows are light and fluffy, they can easily blow around and possibly blow up into the heating element. If you want to have a marshmallow topping, consider using the jarred marshmallow fluff, or push the marshmallows into the casserole so that they don't fly around while air frying.

How do I store leftover sweet potato casserole?

Store leftover sweet potato casserole in an airtight container in the refrigerator for up to 4 days.

How do I reheat leftover air fryer sweet potato casserole?

To reheat leftover casserole, add it to an oven-safe dish and reheat in the air fryer at 350 degrees Fahrenheit for 2-3 minutes, or until the casserole is heated through.

What are additions I can make to sweet potato casserole?

You can change the flavors in sweet potato casserole by adding different ingredients such as diced pineapple. It gives the casserole an even more pronounced flavor and it is delicious!

Air Fryer Diced Potatoes

Servings: 4
Cooking Time: 20 Minutes

Ingredients:
- 1 ½ pounds of small potatoes
- 2 cups cold water
- 1 tablespoon fresh thyme or 1 teaspoon dried thyme
- ½ tablespoon minced garlic
- ½ tablespoon olive oil
- Juice of 1/2 a lemon, about 2 tablespoons of a medium size lemon
- Salt to taste

Directions:
1. Wash your potatoes and dice them into small cubes. The closer they are in size, the more evenly they will cook.
2. Soak the cut potatoes for 10 minutes in cold water. This will help remove some starch and allow them to crisp up more. Once they have soaked, drain them and then pat them dry with a paper towel.
3. Combine potatoes with the thyme, garlic, olive oil and lemon juice.
4. Place diced potatoes in your air fryer basket. Cook at 380 degrees F for 20 to 25 minutes, giving the basket a good shake at the 10 minute mark.

NOTES
OPTIONAL

Sprinkle more fresh thyme to the potatoes before serving or some zest from your lemon, or both!

HOW TO REHEAT DICED POTATOES IN THE AIR FRYER

Preheat the air fryer to 350 degrees F.
Lay the leftover diced potatoes in the air fryer basket in a single layer.
Cook for 3 to 5 minutes until heated through.

Air Fryer Kielbasa

Servings: 4
Cooking Time: 8 Minutes

Ingredients:
- 1 package Kielbasa 15 ounces

Directions:
1. To make this kielbasa dish, remove sausage from packaging, and then cut into bite-size pieces (about ½ inch sized coin size pieces.)
2. Transfer to the air fryer basket, and air fry at 380 degrees F for 8-10 minutes. I tossed the pieces of sausage halfway through air frying.
3. Remove from basket and serve!

NOTES

How to Air Fry Frozen Kielbasa

If you want to make this from frozen, place it in the air fryer basket, and air fry at 380 degrees F, for 10-12 minutes cooking time.

FAVORITE AIR FRYER RECIPES

Air Fryer Bratwurst

Servings: 5
Cooking Time: 15 Minutes

Ingredients:
- 1 pound uncooked bratwurst
- 5 hoagie rolls optional
- toppings for serving dijon mustard, sauerkraut, pickles, etc

Directions:
1. Preheat the air fryer to 360°F.
2. Place the brats in a single layer in the air fryer basket.
3. Cook them for 8 minutes, then flip and cook for an additional 5-6 minutes or until they reach an internal temperature of 165°F.
4. Serve in rolls and/or with desired toppings.

Notes
Ensure brats reach an internal temperature of 165°F.
Do not pierce the brats before cooking or they will lose their juices. Use caution when checking the temperature, they can squirt hot liquid when pierced.
Allow brats to cool for a few minutes before serving or topping.

Air Fryer French Bread Pizzas

Servings: 2
Cooking Time: 10 Minutes

Ingredients:
- 1 French bread loaf
- 1/2 cup (120 ml) pizza sauce or tomato sauce
- 1/3 cup (40 g) shredded cheese
- salt , to taste
- black pepper , to taste
- OPTIONAL TOPPINGS
- Pepperoni, cooked Sausage, Bacon pieces, diced Ham, sliced or diced Tomatoes, Mushrooms, Pineapple, etc.
- OTHER SAUCE OPTIONS
- BBQ Sauce, Salsa, White (Alfredo) Sauce, Pesto, etc.
- EQUIPMENT
- Air Fryer
- Air Fryer Rack optional

Directions:
1. Cut French bread loaf to fit the length of your air fryer. Slice in half lengthwise.
2. Lightly spray both sides for an extra crispy crust. Place in air fryer basket/tray with the bottom (crust) side up (only cook in a single layer - cook the pizzas in batches if needed). Air Fry at 360°F/182°C about 2 minutes.
3. Flip the bread, add sauce & toppings.
4. Cover toppings with an air fryer rack to keep toppings from flying around.
5. Air Fry 360°F/182°C for 2-4 minutes or until heated through and cheese is melted. Try air frying for about 2 minutes first. If you want the top to be crispier, add additional minute or two until the pizza is crispy and cheese is melted.
6. Allow pizza to cool for about 2 minutes. Serve warm.

Air Fryer Sausage Rolls

Servings: 12
Cooking Time: 10 Minutes

Ingredients:
- Air Fryer Sausage Rolls
- 3 sausages Note 1
- 3 sheets puff pastry
- 1 tbsp sesame seeds
- 1 eggs

Directions:
1. Air Fryer Sausage Rolls
2. Turn the air fryer on to 180°C/350 F for 15 mins
3. Use a knife and chopping board to remove the casing from the sausages
4. Add egg to a small bowl, pierce yoke and whisk
5. Place a sheet of puff pastry (thawed) onto the chopping board and place 1 off the sausages on top

6. Roll the pastry around the sausage, then use a pastry brush to coat the top of the pastry where the 2 bits of pastry will meet
7. Continue to roll the pastry around the sausage and again brush one side of where the pastry joins with the egg
8. Repeat for each sausage
9. Brush the top of the length of the long rolled sausage with egg
10. Sprinkle the top with sesame seeds
11. Use a knife to cut the excess pastry off each end
12. Then cut the long sausage roll into 4 smaller rolls
13. Spray the Air Fryer Basket with oil (or use baking paper) then place raw sausage rolls into Air Fryer (work in batches)
14. Cook sausage rolls in Air Fryer for 7-9 mins until pastry is golden and crispy
15. Serve with sauce

Air-fryer White Pizza

Servings: 4
Cooking Time: 6 Minutes

Ingredients:
- 1 recipe Food Processor Pizza Dough
- 2 tablespoon olive oil
- ¾ cup whole milk ricotta cheese
- 1 cup shredded mozzarella cheese (4 oz.)
- 1 teaspoon crushed red pepper
- ½ teaspoon sea salt flakes
- 2 tablespoon chopped fresh basil
- Honey (optional)
- Food Processor Pizza Dough
- Olive oil or nonstick cooking spray
- 2 cup all-purpose flour
- 1 package active dry yeast
- 1 teaspoon sugar
- ½ teaspoon salt
- 1 tablespoon olive oil
- ⅔ cup warm water (105°F to 115°F)

Directions:
1. Preheat air fryer at 375°F. Divide Food Processor Pizza Dough into four 4-oz. portions. On a lightly floured surface, roll one portion of dough into an 8-inch circle. Prick all over with a fork. Place in air-fryer basket and cook 3 minutes. Remove from basket and place, top side down, on work surface.
2. Drizzle crust lightly with 1 1/2 tsp. of the oil and spread with 3 Tbsp. of the ricotta cheese. Sprinkle with 1/4 cup of the mozzarella cheese, 1/4 tsp. of the crushed red pepper, and 1/8 tsp. of the salt. Return pizza to air-fryer basket and cook 3 to 4 minutes or until cheese is melted and golden. Repeat with remaining dough and toppings.
3. Before serving, sprinkle pizzas with basil and, if desired, drizzle with honey.
4. Food Processor Pizza Dough
5. Coat a medium bowl with nonstick cooking spray; set aside. In a food processor combine flour, yeast, sugar, and salt. With the food processor running, add olive oil and warm water. Process until a dough forms. Remove and shape into a smooth ball. Place dough in the prepared bowl; turn once to coat dough surface. Cover bowl with plastic wrap. Let stand in a warm place until doubled in size (45 to 60 minutes).

*Tip
For a delicious garlic-herb crust, add 1 Tbsp. dried Italian seasoning, crushed, and 2 cloves garlic, minced, to the flour mixture when preparing the dough.

*Make-Ahead Directions:
At this point, the dough portions can be placed in a storage container that has been lightly coated with nonstick cooking spray or brushed with olive oil. Cover and store in the refrigerator for up to 24 hours. Or place each dough portion in a freezer bag that has been lightly coated with nonstick cooking spray or brushed with olive oil. Seal, label, and freeze up to 3 months. Thaw in the refrigerator before using.

Air Fryer Frozen Corn Dogs

Servings: 5
Cooking Time: 10 Minutes

Ingredients:
- 5 frozen corn dogs

Directions:
1. Preheat your air fryer to 350 degrees.
2. Place the frozen corn dogs into the air fryer and cook for 10-13 minutes, checking the inside with an Instant Read Thermometer.
3. Remove the corn dogs from the air fryer and enjoy!

NOTES
HOW TO REHEAT CORN DOGS IN AN AIR FRYER:
Preheat your air fryer to 400 degrees.
Cook the corn dogs in the air fryer for 3-5 minutes, remove them from the air fryer, and enjoy!

Air Fryer Mini Corn Dogs

Servings: 4
Cooking Time: 8 Minutes

Ingredients:
- 20 mini corn dogs frozen
- toppings Ketchup, mustard

Directions:
1. Place the mini corn dogs into the air fryer basket, without stacking or overlapping. If you have a smaller basket, air fry 10 at a time.
2. Air fry at 380 degrees F for 9-11 minutes, or until corn dogs reach your desired crispness and the hot dog in the middle is cooked.
3. Serve with your favorite toppings.

NOTES
I make this recipe in my Cosori 8 qt. air fryer or 6.8 quart air fryer. Depending on your air fryer, size and wattages, cooking time may need to be adjusted 1-2 minutes.

Char Siu Dinner

Servings: 5

Ingredients:
- Marinade:
- 1 teaspoon five-spice powder
- 2 teaspoons kosher salt
- ¼ teaspoon ground white pepper
- 4 tablespoons granulated sugar
- 1½ tablespoons soy sauce
- 2 tablespoons hoisin sauce
- 1 tablespoon Chinese rice wine
- 2 tablespoons honey
- 2 garlic cloves, minced
- 2 cubes red fermented bean curd, mashed
- 3 teaspoons red fermented bean curd liquid
- Pork:
- 2 pounds Boston butt (pork shoulder), tops and sides scored
- 3 tablespoons honey
- Oil spray
- For Serving:
- 2 cups short grain white rice, steamed
- 1 cup Taiwanese cabbage, sauteed, for serving
- Items Needed:
- Pastry brush

Directions:
1. Combine marinade ingredients in a large bowl and mix until well combined. Set 4 tablespoons of marinade aside in the refrigerator.
2. Remove the thick, fatty pork rinds from around the entire piece of pork shoulder.
3. Slice the pork into smaller pieces, about 2-cm long and ¾-inch thick.
4. Place the pork and marinade into a large resealable plastic bag and shake until fully coated. Marinate for 1-2 days in the refrigerator.
5. Rest the pork for 30 minutes at room temperature before cooking.
6. Select the Preheat function on the Air Fryer, adjust temperature to 400°F, and press Start/Pause.
7. Mix the honey, 1½ tablespoons of water, and the 4 tablespoons of reserved marinade in a small bowl to make a basting mixture.

8. Spray the inner basket of the air fryer with oil spray.
9. Brush both sides of the pork slices with the basting mixture, then place into the preheated air fryer.

Note: The pieces pork can be touching each other, but should not be stacked on top of each other. You may need to work in batches. Set temperature to 400°F and time to 12 minutes, press Shake, then press Start/Pause.

Flip the pork pieces over and brush more of the basting mixture on each side halfway through cooking. The Shake Reminder will let you know when.

Remove the pork when done, then transfer to a wire rack.

Baste the top of the pork with the remaining basting mixture.

Serve the Char Siu over steamed white rice with a side of sautéed Taiwanese cabbage.

Air Fryer Flatbread Pizzas

Servings: 2
Cooking Time: 10 Minutes

Ingredients:
- 2 pre-cooked flatbread or naan
- 1/2 cup (120 ml) pizza sauce or tomato sauce
- 1/3 cup (40 g) shredded cheese
- salt , to taste
- black pepper , to taste
- OPTIONAL TOPPINGS
- Pepperoni, cooked Sausage, Bacon pieces, diced Ham, sliced or diced Tomatoes, Mushrooms, Pineapple, etc.
- OTHER SAUCE OPTIONS
- BBQ Sauce, Salsa, White (Alfredo) Sauce, Pesto, etc.
- EQUIPMENT
- Air Fryer
- Air Fryer Rack optional

Directions:
1. Place the flatbreads (naan) in air fryer bottom side up (make sure it is in just a single layer - cook in batches if needed).
2. Air Fry at 360°F/182°C about 2-3 minutes. Flip the flatbreads over. Continue to Air fry at 360°F/182°C for another 1-2 minutes (if you want the crust extra crispy - air fry each side a couple minutes more).
3. Divide the sauce between the toasted flatbreads. Top with cheese and add additional salt, pepper and other preferred toppings.
4. To keep your topping from flying around, place an air fryer rack over the flatbread pizzas.
5. Air Fry the pizzas at 360°F/182°C for 2-5 minutes or until heated through and cheese is melted.

Air Fryer Brats

Servings: 6
Cooking Time: 7 Minutes

Ingredients:
- 6 bratwurst uncooked
- 1 serving cooking spray

Directions:
1. Preheat the air fryer to 150C/300F. Spray oil in an air fryer basket.
2. Add the bratwurst in a single layer in the air fryer basket.
3. Cook for 8-10 minutes, flipping halfway through.

Notes
TO STORE: Place leftovers in the refrigerator, covered, for up to 5 days.
TO FREEZE: Place the cooked and cooled brats in a ziplock bag and store it in the freezer for up to two months.
TO REHEAT: Reheat the bratwurst in the microwave, non-stick pan, or air fryer.

Buttermilk Ranch Dressing

Servings: 16

Ingredients:
- 1 cup buttermilk
- ⅔ cup mayonnaise (I use low fat)
- ⅔ cup sour cream (I use low fat)
- 1 tablespoon fresh chives chopped
- 1 tablespoon fresh dill chopped
- 1 tablespoon fresh parsley chopped

- ¾ teaspoon garlic powder
- ¾ teaspoon onion powder
- ½ teaspoon salt & pepper (each)

Directions:
1. Mix all ingredients in a bowl.
2. Refrigerate at least 30 minutes before serving.
3. Notes
4. Reduce buttermilk to ¾ cup to make ranch dip.
5. If using dried herbs, use 1 teaspoon of each (instead of 1 tablespoon).
6. Keeps 1 week in the fridge.

Air Fryer Cacio E Pepe Spaghetti Squash

Servings: 2

Ingredients:
- 1 medium spaghetti squash (about 2 lb.), halved lengthwise
- 2 tbsp. extra-virgin olive oil, plus more for drizzling
- 2 tbsp. grated Parmesan, plus more for serving
- 3/4 tsp. kosher salt
- 1/2 tsp. freshly ground black pepper, plus more
- Torn fresh basil leaves, torn, for serving

Directions:
1. In an air-fryer basket, arrange one-half of squash cut side down. Cook at 360° until squash is tender and golden, 20 to 25 minutes. Repeat with other half of squash.
2. Scrape and fluff insides of squash with a fork and transfer to a medium bowl; reserve shells for serving, if desired. Add oil, Parmesan, salt, and 1/2 teaspoon pepper to bowl and toss to combine.
3. Stuff insides back into reserved shells or divide between plates. Drizzle with more oil. Top with more Parmesan, pepper, and basil.

Air Fryer Grilled Cheese And Ham Crescent Pockets

Servings: 4

Ingredients:
- 1 can (8 oz) refrigerated Pillsbury™ Original Crescent Rolls (8 Count) or 1 can (8 oz) refrigerated Pillsbury™ Original Crescent Dough Sheet
- 4 slices (0.8 oz each) Swiss cheese, cut in half (from 7-oz package)
- 4 slices (4 oz) cooked deli ham (from 7-oz package)

Directions:
1. Cut two 8-inch rounds of cooking parchment paper. Place round in bottom of air fryer basket. Spray with cooking spray.
2. If using crescent rolls, separate dough into 4 rectangles; reshape each rectangle to form 6x4-inch rectangle, firmly pressing perforations to seal; if using dough sheet, unroll and cut into 4 (6x4-inch) rectangles.
3. Place one cheese slice half on center of each rectangle to within 1/2 inch of edge. Top each with 1 slice ham (folding in half to fit), and top with another cheese slice half. Fold dough from top over cheese and ham; firmly press edges with fork to seal. Place two filled crescents onto parchment round in basket of air fryer, spacing apart.
4. Set air fryer to 325°F; bake 8 to 10 minutes or until deep golden brown on top and sturdy enough to turn over with tongs. With tongs or spatula, carefully turn over crescents, and bake 3 to 6 minutes longer or until dough is deep golden brown and thoroughly cooked. Cover loosely with foil to keep warm while baking second batch. Repeat for remaining filled crescents, and place on remaining parchment round in basket of air fryer. Bake as directed as above.

Air Fryer Fried Brown Rice

Servings: 2

Ingredients:
- 1 large carrot, peeled, trimmed, and chopped into small pieces (about 3/4 c.)
- 2 scallions, thinly sliced, white and green parts separated
- 2 tsp. finely chopped fresh ginger (from a 1" piece)
- 1 tbsp. vegetable oil
- 1/4 tsp. kosher salt
- 2 c. long-grain brown rice
- 1 clove garlic, finely chopped
- 2 1/2 tsp. low-sodium soy sauce
- 2 tsp. toasted sesame oil
- Freshly ground black pepper
- 1 large egg, lightly beaten
- 1/2 c. frozen peas, thawed

Directions:
1. In a 7" nonstick round pan, combine carrot, white scallion parts, ginger, vegetable oil, and salt. In an air-fryer basket, place pan. Cook at 400°, stirring halfway through, until onion and carrot are just tender, about 5 minutes.
2. Remove air-fryer basket and add rice, garlic, soy sauce, sesame oil, and a few grinds of pepper to carrot mixture; stir to combine. Continue to cook at 400° until rice is lightly toasted, about 5 minutes more.
3. Remove air-fryer basket and pour egg over half of rice mixture and peas over other half. Continue to cook at 400° until egg is just set and peas are warm, about 4 minutes more; stir to combine. Top with green scallion parts.

Air Fryer Totino's Pizza

Servings: 4
Cooking Time: 6 Minutes

Ingredients:
- 1 Totino's Party Pizza

Directions:
1. Remove the frozen pizza from packaging. Lightly spray the air fryer tray or air fryer basket with an air fryer safe cooking spray.
2. Place pizza in basket. No need to preheat air fryer. Air fry at 400 degrees F for 6-8 minutes, until it has a crispy crust and has reached your desired level of crispiness.
3. Serve while hot.

NOTES
I love this brand of frozen pizza because they have options for pizza toppings. I love pepperoni, or triple cheese pizza. Unless the pizza is deep dish, the cooking times should be the same.

Air Fryer Reheating Leftover Pizza

Servings: 1
Cooking Time: 6 Minutes

Ingredients:
- 1-2 slices leftover pizza
- oil spray , (optional to lightly coat the pizza so toppings don't dry out - need depends on yoout particular toppings)
- EQUIPMENT
- Air Fryer

Directions:
1. Place foil or perforated parchment sheet to base on air fryer basket, rack or tray. Place the pizza on top. If needed, lightly spray the top of pizza so that the toppings don't burn or dry out (optional).
2. Air Fry at 360°F/180°C for 3-6 minutes or until cooked to your desired crispness. If unsure, start cooking for 3 minutes first. Then check to see if it's to your liking. Cook additional minute or two if you want the pizza to be crispier. Deep dish crusts will take a little longer, while thin crust will be slightly quicker.
3. Let the slice of pizza cool for a touch & enjoy!

NOTES
Air Frying Tips and Notes:
Recipe timing is based on a non-preheated air fryer. If cooking in multiple slices back to back, the following slices may cook a little quicker because the air fryer is already hot.
Recipes were tested in 3.7 to 6 qt. air fryers. If using a larger air fryer, the pizza slices might cook quicker so adjust cooking time.

Air Fryer Fried Rice

Ingredients:
- 3 cups rice cooked and cold
- 1 cup frozen mixed vegetables
- 1 tbsp oyster sauce
- 1 tsp sesame oil
- 2 eggs scrambled
- 2 tbsp choppled green onion tops

Directions:
1. To make your air fryer fried rice, put your cold rice into an large bowl.
2. Mix in the frozen vegetables to the bowl of rice.
3. Add the scrambled eggs into the rice and vegetables.
4. Add the sesame oil and oyster sauce. Mix well until fully combined.
5. Transfer the rice mixture to an oven safe container like a ramekin.
6. Place that container into your air fryer. Cook the air fried rice at 360 degrees F for 15 minutes stirring every 5 minutes. Add in the green onion tops during the last minutes of cooking time, stirring them in until well combined.
7. Serve immediately.

Air Fryer Tostones

Servings: 2
Cooking Time: 20 Minutes

Ingredients:
- 1 large green plantain (ends trimmed and peeled (6 oz after))
- olive oil spray (I like Bertolli)
- 1 cup water
- 1 teaspoon kosher salt
- 3/4 teaspoon garlic powder

Directions:
1. With a sharp knife cut a slit along the length of the plantain skin, this will make it easier to peel. Cut the plantain into 1 inch pieces, 8 total.
2. In a small bowl combine the water with salt and garlic powder.
3. Preheat the air fryer to 400F.
4. When ready, spritz the plantain with olive oil and cook 6 minutes, you might have to do this in 2 batches.
5. Remove from the air fryer and while they are hot mash them with a tostonera or the bottom of a jar or measuring cup to flatten.
6. Dip them in the seasoned water and set aside.
7. Preheat the air fryer to 400F once again and cook, in batches 5 minutes on each side, spraying both sides of the plantains with olive oil.
8. When done, give them another spritz of oil and season with salt. Eat right away.

3 Cheese Air Fryer Mini Pizzas

Cooking Time: 4 Minutes

Ingredients:
- 1 can biscuits
- ⅓ cup pizza sauce
- ⅓ cup mozzarella cheese shredded
- ⅓ cup cheddar cheese shredded
- 2 tablespoon parmesan cheese grated

Directions:
1. Preheat air fryer to 400°F.
2. Roll out the biscuits into flat circles.
3. Top with the pizza sauce and cheese.
4. Place in the air fryer basket and cook for 4 minutes or until cheese is melted.

Air Fryer Hot Pockets

Servings: 1
Cooking Time: 12 Minutes

Ingredients:
- 1 Frozen Hot Pocket
- EQUIPMENT
- Air Fryer

Directions:
1. Place the frozen hot pocket in the air fryer basket. If cooking multiple hot pockets, spread out into a single even layer. No oil spray is needed.
2. Air Fry at 380°F/193°C for 10 minutes. If needed, flip the hot pocket over and cook for another 1-3 minutes or until cooked to

your preference. Cooking more than 1 hot pocket at a time might require more cooking time.

NOTES
Air Frying Tips and Notes:
No Oil Necessary. Cook Frozen - Do not thaw first.
Shake or turn if needed. Don't overcrowd the air fryer basket.
Recipe timing is based on a non-preheated air fryer. If cooking in multiple batches of hot pockets back to back, the following batches may cook a little quicker.
Recipes were tested in 3.7 to 6 qt. air fryers. If using a larger air fryer, the hot pockets might cook quicker so adjust cooking time.

Air Fryer Jalepeno Poppers

Servings: 6
Cooking Time: 12 Minutes

Ingredients:
- 6 medium Jalapeños
- 4 ounces cream cheese, softened
- 6-12 slices bacon

Directions:
1. Cut the jalapeños in half, lengthwise. Remove all of the seeds and rinse the jalapeños.
2. Cut small slices of the cream cheese, in strips, and place a strip inside each half piece of the pepper.
3. Wrap a piece of bacon around the stuffed pepper and secure with a toothpick.
4. Place the stuffed peppers in the basket of the air fryer, working in batches if necessary. Be sure they aren't overlapping each other in the basket.
5. Cook at 370 degrees Fahrenheit for 10-12 minutes, until the bacon is cooked to your desired crispness.

NOTES
If you use smaller jalapeños, cut the bacon slices in half before wrapping the pepper. If the cream cheese is chilled, it is easier to cut into strips.
This recipe makes 12 poppers, with a serving of three poppers per person.

Air Fryer Hot Dogs

Servings: 4
Cooking Time: 8 Minutes

Ingredients:
- 4 hot dogs
- 4 hot dog buns
- Optional toppings: ketchup, relish, mustard, chopped onions

Directions:
1. Heat an air fryer to 375°F.
2. Place 4 hot dogs in a single layer in the air fryer basket. Air fry until the hot dogs look plump and are slightly browned, flipping them halfway through, 5 to 6 minutes total.
3. If you want toasted buns, transfer a hot dog into each bun. Return to the air fryer basket in a single layer and air fry until the buns are toasted, about 2 minutes. Serve with desired toppings.

Air Fryer Frozen Mozzarella Sticks

Servings: 2
Cooking Time: 6 Minutes

Ingredients:
- 10 frozen mozzarella sticks
- marinara sauce or your favorite dipping sauce

Directions:
1. Preheat the air fryer to 360 degrees.
2. Place the frozen mozzarella sticks in the air fryer cook for 6-8 minutes.
3. Pinch slightly (and carefully since they're hot). They are done when the cheese inside is soft and there is give to the mozzarella stick.
4. Remove them from the air fryer and enjoy with a marinara sauce for dipping.

SNACKS & APPETIZERS RECIPES

Air Fryer Frozen French Fries

Servings: 4
Cooking Time: 15 Minutes

Ingredients:
- 1 teaspoon oil
- 250 grams frozen french fries (more or less depending on the size of your air fryer and servings you want)
- 1/4 teaspoon seasoning salt

Directions:
1. Preheat air fryer to 400 degrees for 5 minutes.
2. Meanwhile, toss frozen french fries with seasoning salt.
3. Open the air fryer basket and brush with oil (not totally necessary, but ensures the fries will not stick).
4. Place frozen french fries in air fryer basket in a single layer or as close as possible.
5. Cook at 400 degrees F for 15-20 minutes, checking and stirring every 5 minutes, until crispy.

Curly Fries In The Air Fryer

Servings: 4
Cooking Time: 10 Minutes

Ingredients:
- 1 package of Arby's Seasoned Curly Fries
- Dipping sauce of your choice

Directions:
1. Preheat your air fryer to 400 degrees.
2. Place a single layer of fries, it is okay if they overlap slightly, into the basket.
3. Cook for 8-10 minutes, shaking the basket halfway through, till the desired crispiness.

NOTES
HOW TO REHEAT CURLY FRIES:
Preheat your air fryer.
Add fries to the basket and cook for 3-4 minutes or until hot.

Homemade Chips

Servings: 4

Ingredients:
- 500g white potatoes, cut in 6mm thick by 5cm long sticks
- 1/2-3 tbsp vegetable oil
- COOKING MODE
- When entering cooking mode - We will enable your screen to stay 'always on' to avoid any unnecessary interruptions whilst you cook!

Directions:
1. Soak cut potatoes in cold water for 30 minutes to remove excess starch. Drain well, then pat with a paper towel until very dry
2. Place both ingredients into a large mixing bowl; toss to combine. Use at least 1/2 tablespoon oil. For crispier results, use up to 3 tablespoons oil
3. Insert crisper plate in pan and pan in unit. Preheat unit by selecting AIR FRY, setting the temperature to 200°C and setting the time to 3 minutes. Select START/STOP to begin
4. After 3 minutes, place chips on the crisper plate; reinsert pan. Select AIR FRY, set temperature to 200°C and set time to 25 minutes. Select START/STOP to begin
5. After 10 minutes, remove pan from unit and shake chips or toss them with silicone-tipped tongs. Reinsert pan to resume cooking
6. Check chips after 20 minutes. For crispier chips, continue cooking for up to 25 minutes
7. When cooking is complete, serve immediately with your favourite sauce

Frozen Waffle Fries In The Air Fryer

Servings: 4
Cooking Time: 8 Minutes

Ingredients:
- 1 pound frozen waffle fries (1/2 bag)
- OPTIONAL
- Dipping sauce of choice

Directions:
1. Preheat your air fryer to 400 degrees F.
2. Place a single layer of frozen waffle fries in your air fryer. They can overlap slightly.
3. Cook the fries for 8 to 10 minutes, carefully shaking the basket halfway through cooking.
4. Remove the waffle fries from the air fryer, serve with your favorite dipping sauce, and enjoy!

NOTES
HOW TO REHEAT WAFFLE FRIES IN THE AIR FRYER:
Preheat your air fryer to 350 degrees.
Place your leftover waffle fries in the air fryer and cook for about 2 minutes, until warmed thoroughly.

Air Fryer Home Fries
Servings: 4
Cooking Time: 40 Minutes

Ingredients:
- 1 tablespoon olive oil
- 1 ½ pounds russet potatoes
- ½ teaspoon seasoned salt
- ½ teaspoon garlic powder
- ¼ cup onion chopped
- ¼ cup bell pepper red or green, chopped
- 1 tablespoon melted butter

Directions:
1. Peel potatoes (if desired) and cut into ½" chunks.
2. Toss potatoes with olive oil, seasoned salt & garlic powder.
3. Add to the air fryer basket and cook at 380°F for 15 minutes.
4. Combine onion, bell pepper and butter. Add to the air fryer, reduce heat to 340°F and cook an additional 15 minutes or until vegetables and potatoes are tender.
5. Serve immediately.

Notes
Store leftover home fries in the fridge in an airtight container for up to 4 days.
To reheat, put in the microwave for a minute or two or place back in the air fryer for 5 minutes or until heated through.

Air Fryer Green Beans
Cooking Time: 8 Minutes

Ingredients:
- 1 lb Green beans (trimmed)
- 6 cloves Garlic (minced)
- 1/2 tsp Sea salt
- 1/4 tsp Black pepper
- 2 tbsp Olive oil
- 1 tbsp Lemon juice

Directions:
1. Preheat the air fryer to 375 degrees F (191 degrees C).
2. In a large bowl, combine all the ingredients.
3. Arrange green beans in the air fryer basket, in a single layer.
4. Cook green beans in the air fryer for 7-10 minutes, until tender. Shake the basket halfway through the cook time.

Air Fryer Green Bean Fries
Servings: 4
Cooking Time: 5 Minutes

Ingredients:
- 1 pound green beans fresh
- 1 cup Parmesan cheese
- 1 cup panko bread crumbs
- 1 Tablespoon garlic powder
- 2 eggs
- 1/2 cup all purpose flour
- 2 Tablespoons Olive oil spray

Directions:
1. Preheat Air Fryer to 390 degrees Fahrenheit (199 degrees Celcius).
2. Snap the ends off the fresh green beans, then place them into a colander to rinse. Place the green beans on a paper towel and pat dry.
3. Coat the green beans in the all purpose flour.
4. Whisk together the eggs in a small bowl.
5. Mix together parmesan cheese, panko breadcrumbs, and garlic powder in a separate bowl.

6. Dip the green beans into the egg mixture, and then dip the green beans into the panko and cheese mixture.
7. Coat the green beans well. Add the green beans to a cooling rack as you work to finish the remainder of the green beans. Spray the coated beans with a light coating of olive oil.
8. Place the coated green beans in the Air Fryer basket and air fry for 5 minutes or until golden brown.
9. Sprinkle with additional parmesan cheese or fresh lemon juice if desired and serve with your favorite dipping sauce.

NOTES

Arrange your green beans in a single layer: Spreading your green beans out ensures even cooking through the dish.

Cooking spray: You can use olive oil cooking spray, canola oil spray, or avocado oil spray for this recipe.

Coat the green beans well: Use a bit of the breading mix when coating your green beans. The more breading you have, the crispier your green beans will be.

This recipe was made with a basket-style 5.8 qt Cosori Air Fryer. If you're using a different brand, you may have to adjust your cooking time accordingly.

Air Fryer Zucchini Chips

Servings: 4
Cooking Time: 12 Minutes

Ingredients:
- 1 medium zucchini cut into ½" coins
- 1 beaten egg
- cooking spray
- Crumb Coating
- ⅔ cup Panko bread crumbs
- ⅔ cup seasoned bread crumbs
- 2 tablespoons Parmesan cheese grated
- 1 teaspoon Italian seasoning

Directions:
1. Preheat air fryer to 375°F.
2. Mix coating ingredients in a bowl.
3. Toss zucchini with egg. Dip zucchini into the coating mixture gently pressing to adhere.
4. Lightly spray zucchini with cooking spray.
5. Place in a single layer in the air fryer basket and cook 6 minutes. Turn zucchini over and air fry 6-8 minutes more or until crisp and zucchini is tender.

Notes

For batches, undercook zucchini by 2 minutes. Once all batches are cooked, place them all in the air fryer together for 3 minutes to heat through. Reheat in the air fryer at 375°F for 3-5 minutes or until heated through.

Air Fryer French Fries

Servings: 4
Cooking Time: 25 Minutes

Ingredients:
- 2 russet potatoes
- 1 tablespoon extra virgin olive oil
- 1/8 teaspoon salt

Directions:
1. Fill a medium-sized bowl halfway with cold water
2. Peel potatoes (if desired) and cut them into 1/4 inch slices.
3. As you slice the potatoes, add them into the water to soak
4. Drain potatoes and fill bowl back up. Mix the potatoes around like you're rotating a salad with your hands. Drain again. Repeat 5-6 times until water is clear.
5. Dry off potatoes and bowl with a paper towel
6. Add potatoes back to dry bowl. Add extra virgin olive oil and salt. Mix to combine.
7. Cook french fries at 350 degrees for 10 minutes, then at 400 degrees for 15-18 minutes, shaking the basket every 5 minutes.

Air Fryer Sweet Potato Cubes

Servings: 3
Cooking Time: 10 Minutes

Ingredients:
- 1 large sweet potato, or two medium ones
- 1 tablespoon olive oil
- 1 teaspoon brown sugar (optional)
- ½ teaspoon salt
- ½ teaspoon dried parsley

- Fresh parsley for garnish (optional)

Directions:
1. Preheat your air fryer to 400F.
2. Peel and slice the sweet potato into ½ inch cubes, you should have 2-2 ½ cups sweet potato cubes.
3. Place sweet potato cubes into a large mixing bowl, drizzle with oil and sprinkle seasonings, then toss to combine.
4. Add the seasoned sweet potato to the air fryer, then cook for 8-10 minutes, shaking the basket halfway through.
5. Sprinkle parsley and serve warm.

Air Fried Cheesy Mashed Potato Balls

Ingredients:
- Leftover mashed potatoes
- 1 cup cheese of your choice
- 1 cup green chiles
- Auntie NoNo's Everything Seasoning
- 1/2 cup Flour
- 2 eggs
- 1 cup Panko breadcrumbs

Directions:
1. If you aren't using leftover mashed potatoes, you will need to refrigerate them until they are cold.
2. Add in the cheese, green chiles and a generous amount of Auntie Nono's Everything seasoning to the potatoes and mix until well combined.
3. Preheat the air fryer oven to 350°.
4. Prepare your breading station by putting flour, 2 whisked eggs and the panko bread crumbs in 3 separate bowls and set aside.
5. Using an ice cream scooper, scoop the potatoes into medium sized balls.
6. Dip the balls into the flour, then the egg and lastly, into the bread crumbs.
7. Arrange them all onto the mesh rack accessory and air fry at 350° for 8-9 minutes.
8. Dip these in your favorite dipping sauce and enjoy!

Air Fryer Kale Chips

Servings: 4
Cooking Time: 3 Minutes

Ingredients:
- 1 bunch kale
- 2 teaspoons olive oil
- 1/2 teaspoon salt

Directions:
1. Wash the kale and pat dry until completely dry. Roughly tear the leaves into bite sized pieces.
2. Add the kale to a mixing bowl, then drizzle with olive oil. Using your hands, rub the leaves to ensure they have some oil on them. Sprinkle the salt all over.
3. Transfer the kale to the air fryer basket and air fry at 190C/375F for 3-4 minutes, ensuring they don't burn.
4. Repeat the process until all the kale chips are cooked.

Notes
TO STORE: It's best to store the cooled kale chips in a paper bag at room temperature to prevent them from becoming soggy. They should stay crisp for up to 3 days.

Air Fryer Spicy Onion Rings

Servings: 4
Cooking Time: 10 Minutes

Ingredients:
- 2 large sweet onions, sliced 1/2 inch thick
- Batter:
- ⅔ cup buttermilk
- 1 egg
- ¼ cup all-purpose flour
- 1 teaspoon RedHot Chile and Lime Seasoning Blend (such as Frank's®)
- ½ teaspoon adobo all-purpose seasoning (such as Goya®)
- Breading:
- 2 cups panko bread crumbs
- 1 teaspoon adobo all-purpose seasoning (such as Goya®)
- ½ teaspoon RedHot Chile and Lime Seasoning Blend (such as Frank's®)

- olive oil cooking spray
- 1 teaspoon kosher salt, or to taste

Directions:
1. Whisk together buttermilk, egg, flour, chile and lime seasoning, and adobo seasoning for the batter in a shallow bowl. Cover and refrigerate for 30 minutes.
2. Combine panko, adobo seasoning, and chile and lime seasoning in a shallow dish; mix well. Remove batter from the fridge. Dip onion rings first into the batter, then into bread crumb mixture, turning to coat, and gently shake off excess crumbs. Lightly spritz the onion rings with cooking spray on both sides.
3. Preheat the air fryer to 340 degrees F (170 degrees C). Line the air fryer basket with a parchment liner or lightly spray with oil.
4. Place the breaded onion rings into the fryer basket in an even layer, leaving about 1/2-inch space between the slices.
5. Cook until crisp and lightly browned, flipping halfway through, 10 to 12 minutes. You may have to cook in batches, and cooking time may vary depending on the size and brand of your air fryer.
6. Remove from the air fryer, transfer to a baking sheet, sprinkle with kosher salt, and place in a 250 degrees F (120 degrees C) oven to keep warm.

Cook's Notes:
You can find Chile n' Lime seasoning and Adobo seasoning in the Hispanic section of your supermarket. Adobo should be available at most stores, but if Chile n' Lime is not, use all Adobo. Chilling the batter will make the breading adhere better. You may bread the onion rings, cover early in the day, and refrigerate until ready to cook.

Air Fryer Beet Chips

Servings: 4
Cooking Time: 30 Minutes

Ingredients:
- 3 beets
- 1 Tablespoon olive oil
- 1 teaspoon Kosher salt
- 1 teaspoon ground black pepper

Directions:
1. Carefully peel the beets and then slice them to your desired thickness using a mandolin. (Careful, these are sharp!)
2. Add the sliced beets into a medium sized mixing bowl and then coat with olive oil, salt, and pepper. Mix until the beets are coated evenly.
3. Add the beet chips in a single layer into the basket of the air fryer. It's ok to overlap the beet chips slightly.
4. Air fry beet chips at 320 degrees Fahrenheit for 30 minutes, carefully flipping the beef chips halfway through the cooking process.
5. Start checking on the chips with 5 minutes remaining and pull the chips early if they are browning fast. (This will depend on the size and thickness of the slices.)
6. Remove the beet chips for the air fryer basket and place them on a wire cooling rack for a few minutes before serving.

NOTES
This recipe was made with a 1700 watt basket style 5.8 quart Cosori air fryer. If you are using a different size or different brand of air fryer, you may need to add a minute or two. All air fryers cook a little differently.
Store any leftover beet chips in an airtight container for up to 3 days.
Consider spicing things up by adding a ¼ teaspoon of cayenne pepper, white pepper, or even some red pepper flakes.

Air Fryer Popcorn

Servings: 4
Cooking Time: 8 Minutes

Ingredients:
- 1/2 cup popcorn kernels
- 1 teaspoon salt to serve * See notes

Directions:
1. Preheat the air fryer at 200C/400F for 5 minutes.
2. Line the base of the air fryer basket with tin foil. Place the popcorn kernels in a single layer on top of it.

3. Place the air fryer basket in the air fryer and cook for 8 minutes. Let the popcorn sit in the air fryer for a further 30 seconds, to allow excess popping.
4. Remove the air fryer basket and place the popcorn into a mixing bowl. Toss with salt and your favorite seasonings and enjoy immediately.

Notes

* Flavor options included in the body of the post. TO STORE: Like microwave or stovetop popcorn, air fryer popcorn can be stored at room temperature in a sealed container. The popcorn will remain fresh for up to 1 week.

Air Fryer Sweet Potato Fries

Servings: 4
Cooking Time: 15 Minutes

Ingredients:
- 2 medium sweet potatoes
- 1 tablespoon olive oil
- 1/2 teaspoon fine sea salt
- 1/2 teaspoon garlic powder
- 1/4 teaspoon paprika

Directions:
1. Cut sweet potatoes into 1/2 inch strips to create fries.
2. Coat sweet potato fries with olive oil.
3. Add in the fine sea salt, garlic powder, and paprika and mix to combine seasoning evenly.
4. Cook the sweet potato fries at 380 degrees for 15-18 minutes, shaking the basket every 5 minutes.

NOTES
HOW TO REHEAT SWEET POTATO FRIES IN THE AIR FRYER:
Preheat your air fryer to 350 degrees.
Place your leftover sweet potato fries in the air fryer and cook for about 3 to 5 minutes, until warmed and crisped.

Air Fryer Nachos

Servings: 4
Cooking Time: 1 Minutes

Ingredients:
- 2 cups Green Mountain Gringo® Original Tortilla Strips
- 1/2 cup Green Mountain Gringo® Medium Salsa
- 1/3 cup canned black beans, drained and rinsed
- 1/4 teaspoon lime juice
- 1/2 cup Mexican cheese
- 1 avocado, diced
- 2 green onions, chopped
- Sour cream, for drizzling

Directions:
1. Press a piece of aluminum foil down into your air fryer to form a flat bottom. Make sure the sides go up the air fryer at least 2 inches (so you can safely remove the nachos after heating). Remove foil from air fryer keeping its form.
2. Preheat your air fryer to 370 degrees.
3. Add chips to the aluminum foil then add salsa, black beans, and lime juice on top. Sprinkle cheese across the top of the nachos.
4. Carefully place the nachos inside the air fryer and cook for 1-2 minutes, until cheese is just melted.
5. Remove nachos from the air fryer and top with avocados, green onions, and sour cream.
6. Enjoy immediately.

NOTES
To reheat nachos:
Cook nachos in a preheated air fryer at 320 degrees for 2-3 minutes until warmed thoroughly.
To grill:
Place nachos on grill heated to approximately 350 degrees and cook for 1 minute with the grill closed.
To add ground beef:
Cook 1 quarter pound of ground beef in a pan on medium heat until browned. Drain any liquid, then add 3 teaspoons of taco seasoning and 1 tablespoon of water. Cook for another 1-2

minutes, then add to nachos prior to air frying/grilling.

Easy Onion Rings
Servings: 2
Cooking Time: 10-30 Minutes
Ingredients:
- 1 large onion, sliced into rings about 1.5cm/⅝in thick
- 4 tbsp plain flour
- 1 free-range egg
- 1 tbsp milk (dairy or unsweetened non-dairy)
- 60g/2¼oz panko breadcrumbs
- cooking oil spray
- salt and freshly ground black pepper

Directions:
1. Preheat the oven to 200C/180C Fan/Gas 6, or the air fryer to 180C.
2. Carefully separate the onion slices into rings; some rings should be one onion-layer thick, others two layers.
3. Put half the flour in a shallow bowl and season with salt and pepper. Put the remaining flour in another shallow bowl and whisk in the egg and milk to make a smooth batter. Put the panko breadcrumbs in another shallow bowl.
4. Dip the onion rings into the seasoned flour, making sure they are thoroughly coated all over. Lightly tap off excess flour. Put the floured rings into the batter and flip a few times to coat completely, shaking off excess batter. Finally add them to the breadcrumbs and press crumbs all over them.
5. Spray a baking sheet or the inside of your air fryer with cooking oil. Add the onion rings in a single layer – if air frying you'll need to do them in batches. Spray the tops of the onion rings with more oil.
6. Bake in the oven for 18–20 minutes, turning after 8–10 minutes. Air-fry for 10 minutes, turning halfway through. Keep the first batches of air fryer onion rings warm in a low oven while you cook the rest, then serve immediately.

Air Fryer Turnip Fries
Servings: 4
Cooking Time: 15 Minutes
Ingredients:
- 1 tbs olive oil
- 500g turnips, peeled and sliced into fries
- 1/2 tsp garlic powder
- 1/2 tsp smoked paprika

Directions:
1. Add the turnip fries, olive oil and seasonings to a large bowl and toss well to coat.
2. Place in the air fryer basket and cook for 8 minutes at 200°C, toss and cook for 5 minutes more, until crisp.

Air-fryer Pineapple Chips
Servings: 4
Cooking Time: 1 Hr
Ingredients:
- 1/2 pineapple, skin removed

Directions:
1. Slice pineapple into 2mm-thick slices. Pat dry with paper towel.
2. Preheat air fryer to 140°C for 2 minutes. Working in 4 batches, place fruit, in a single layer, in basket. Cook for 15 minutes, turning halfway through cooking, or until fruit is dry and crisp. Serve.

Air Fryer Potato Skins
Servings: 4
Cooking Time: 11 Minutes
Ingredients:
- 4 medium baked potatoes cooled
- 1 tablespoon oil
- ¼ teaspoon salt or to taste
- 1 cup cheddar cheese
- 2 tablespoons bacon bits
- 1 green onion sliced
- sour cream for serving

Directions:
1. Preheat air fryer to 400°F.
2. Cut baked potatoes in half lengthwise. Use a small spoon to scoop out the flesh, leaving

a ¼" shell. Set potato flesh aside for another use.
3. Brush both sides of the potato skins with oil and season with salt.
4. Place potato skins cut side down on the air fryer tray. Air fry for 7-9 minutes or until crisp, flipping halfway.
5. Sprinkle potato skins with cheese and bacon bits. Return to air fryer and cook for an additional 2 minutes or until cheese is melted and bubbly.
6. Top with green onion and serve with sour cream.

Air Fryer Chickpeas Recipe
Servings: 4
Cooking Time: 13 Minutes

Ingredients:
- 1 14 oz Canned chickpeas
- 1 teaspoon smoked paprika or as needed
- ½ teaspoon onion powder
- ¼ teaspoon Cayenne pepper
- 1 Tablespoon Olive oil

Directions:
1. Preheat the oven at 190C/380F for 3 minutes
2. Open the can of chickpeas, drain in a colander and rinse under a cold running water. Make sure the chickpea is drained completely, alternatively dry in with a kitchen towel or paper.
3. In a bowl, combine the drained chickpeas, smoked paprika, onion powder, cayenne pepper, salt, olive oil and mix to combine
4. Pour the seasoned chickpeas in the air fryer basket and spread it out. Cook for 12 to 15 minutes shaking every 5 minutes or so at 190C/390F or until crispy to your liking. Leave to cool for about 5 minutes and serve. Enjoy!

NOTES
If you like the chickpeas to be soft in the middle then cook it for a lesser time. You can start checking from 10 minutes until the desired texture is achieved.

If time is not of the essence, then you can marinate the chickpeas in the spices for about 10 to 15 minutes before air frying.
While it is tempting to cook the chickpeas at 200C/400F, I would advise against it as it would require shaking more often and might even burn easily too.
Store the chickpea at room temperature
Chickpeas vary in size and that is due to the type of brands you choose, if your legume is on the big side, then you may need to cook it longer than 13 minutes. Start checking from 10 minutes for optimum results.
Do not cook more than 1 can of chickpeas at once in the air fryer to allow for even cooking. Cook in batches if need be.

Air Fryer Frozen Crinkle Cut Fries
Servings: 4
Cooking Time: 12 Minutes

Ingredients:
- 1 lb. (454 g) Frozen crinkle cut fries
- salt , to taste
- black pepper , to taste
- EQUIPMENT
- Air Fryer

Directions:
1. Place the frozen crinkle fries in the air fryer basket and spread out evenly. No oil spray is needed for the fries. It's already been deep fried in oil, so that's enough to air fry.
2. Air Fry at 400°F/205°C for 10-14 minutes. Shake and gently stir about halfway through cooking. If cooking larger batches, or if your fries don't cook evenly, try turning them multiple times on following batches.
3. Want the fries crisper? If needed air fry for an additional 1-3 minutes or until crisped to your liking. Season with salt & pepper, if desired.

NOTES
Air Frying Tips and Notes:
No Oil Necessary. Cook Frozen - Do not thaw first.
Shake or turn if needed. Don't overcrowd the air fryer basket.

Recipe timing is based on a non-preheated air fryer. If cooking in multiple batches of fries back to back, the following batches may cook a little quicker.

Recipes were tested in 3.7 to 6 qt. air fryers. If using a larger air fryer, the fries might cook quicker so adjust cooking time.

Remember to set a timer to shake/flip/toss as directed in recipe.

Air Fryer Keto Onion Rings Recipe

Servings: 4
Cooking Time: 16 Minutes

Ingredients:
- 1 large Onion (sliced into rings 1/2 inch thick)
- 3 tbsp Wholesome Yum Coconut Flour
- 1/4 tsp Sea salt
- 2 large Eggs
- 2/3 cup Pork rinds (~1.8 oz)
- 3 tbsp Wholesome Yum Blanched Almond Flour
- 1/2 tsp Paprika
- 1/2 tsp Garlic powder

Directions:
1. Arrange 3 small, shallow bowls in a line:
2. Coconut flour and sea salt, stirred together
3. Eggs, beaten
4. Pork rinds, almond flour, paprika, and garlic powder, stirred together
5. Lightly grease 2 air fryer oven racks or an air fryer basket.
6. Dredge an onion ring in coconut flour. Dip it in the egg, shake off the excess, then place in the pork rind mixture. Scoop extra pork rind mixture over it, so that it's coated on all size. Place into the air fryer rack or basket. Repeat with all the onion rings, placing them in a single layer without touching. (You may need to cook them in two batches if you don't have 2 air fryer racks.)
7. Preheat the air fryer or air fryer oven to 400 degrees F for 2 to 3 minutes.
8. For an air fryer oven: Place both racks into the air fryer oven. Bake for about 8 minutes, until the top layer is golden. Switch racks and bake for 8 more minutes, until the top layer is golden again.
9. For a regular air fryer: Only half the onion rings will fit into the basket in a single layer. Place the basket into the air fryer. Bake for 16 minutes, until golden. Remove the onion rings, arrange the next batch of uncooked rings, and repeat.

Printed in Great Britain
by Amazon